Ask any survivor of male violence about her abusive experiences and you will undoubtedly discover that she will call for a definition that includes many harmful nonphysical and nonsexual behaviors like those described in this book. It is a vital resource for anyone seeking a richer social scientific understanding of one of the most significant threats to the health and well-being of women today.

Walter DeKeseredy, Director of the Research Center on Violence and Professor of Sociology, West Virginia University

While many countries have criminalised coercive control in order to combat violence against women, fewer have appraised whether such laws will work as promised. In this thoroughgoing critique, Barlow and Walklate offer a radically new perspective that explores how professional responses to victimized women expose them to further jeopardy in the criminal and family courts, child protection systems and from perpetrators themselves. Essential reading that cautions against quick fixes while advising on what needs to be done to best support those facing multiple forms of discrimination and abuse.

David Gadd, Professor of Criminology, University of Manchester

This book is a clear and lucid explanation of the concept of coercive control, as well as some of the central debates and issues thrown up by the research grappling with intimate partner violence in the law and policy context. It is essential reading for academics and policy makers working on improving our responses to intimate partner violence.

Julia Tolmie, Professor of Law, University of Auckland

Coercive Control

This book offers a critical appreciation of the nature and impact of coercive control in interpersonal relationships. It examines what this concept means, who is impacted by the behaviours it captures, and how academics, policymakers, and policy advocates have responded to the increasing recognition of the deleterious effects that coercive control has on especially women's lives.

The book discusses the historical emergence of this concept, who its main proponents have been, and how its effects have been understood. It considers the role of coercive control in making sense of women's pathway into crime as well as their experiences of it as victims. Coercive control has been presented predominantly as a gendered process, and consideration is given in this book to the efficacy of this assumption as well as the extent to which the concept makes sense for a wide constituency of marginalized women. In recent years, much energy has been given to efforts to criminalize coercive control, and the concerns that these efforts generate are discussed in detail, alongside what the limitations to such initiatives might be. In conclusion, the book situates the rising pre-occupation with coercive control within the broader concerns with policy transfer, ways of taking account of victim-survivor voices, alongside the importance of working towards more holistic policy responses to violence(s) against women.

The book will be of particular interest to academics, policymakers, and practitioners working in criminal justice who wish to understand both the nature and extent of coercive control and the importance of appreciating the role of nuance in translating that understanding into practice.

Charlotte Barlow is a Reader in Criminal Justice and Policing at UCLAN. She has led various research projects in the field of domestic abuse, including police responses to coercive control, responding to domestic abuse in rural communities, and victim-survivor experiences of Clare's Law/Domestic Violence Disclosure Schemes.

Sandra Walklate is Eleanor Rathbone Chair of Sociology at the University of Liverpool, UK, conjoint Chair of Criminology, Monash University, Australia. Internationally recognized for her work in victimology, gender, and violence, she is currently President of the British Society of Criminology.

Criminology in Focus

Series Editor: Sandra Walklate

This series offers a space for a 'short format' book series, which showcases and puts the spotlight on new research in criminology. We are interested in books that fit the 'short-form' model; for example: theoretical think pieces, developments in criminal justice policy, paradigm shifting innovations in the fields, a compelling case study that would be of interest to an international readership. We would like to attract 'big names' as well as up-and-coming scholars; all books should speak and contribute to international criminological debates and conversations.

Coercive Control

Charlotte Barlow and Sandra Walklate

Routledge
Taylor & Francis Group

LONDON AND NEW YORK

First published 2022
by Routledge
4 Park Square, Milton Park, Abingdon, Oxon OX14 4RN

and by Routledge
605 Third Avenue, New York, NY 10158

Routledge is an imprint of the Taylor & Francis Group, an informa business

© 2022 Charlotte Barlow and Sandra Walklate

British Library Cataloguing-in-Publication Data
A catalogue record for this book is available from the British Library

Library of Congress Cataloging-in-Publication Data
Names: Barlow, Charlotte, author. | Walklate, Sandra, author.
Title: Coercive control / Charlotte Barlow and Sandra Walklate.
Description: Milton Park, Abingdon, Oxon ;
New York, NY : Routledge, 2022. |
Includes bibliographical references and index. |
Identifiers: LCCN 2021054024 | ISBN 9780367894269 (hardback) |
ISBN 9781003019114 (ebook)
Subjects: LCSH: Criminal anthropology. | Criminal behavior. |
Control (Psychology) | Female offenders–Psychology.
Classification: LCC HV6035 .B37 2022 | DDC 364.2/4–dc23/eng/20211122
LC record available at https://lccn.loc.gov/2021054024

ISBN: 978-0-367-89426-9 (hbk)
ISBN: 978-1-032-22800-6 (pbk)
ISBN: 978-1-003-01911-4 (ebk)

DOI: 10.4324/9781003019114

Typeset in Times New Roman
by Newgen Publishing UK

Contents

Acknowledgements

This book was written during a time in which policy debates in relation to coercive control were reaching a crescendo. This was the case particularly in different states in Australia concerning whether there is a role for the criminal law in responding to coercive control. In many ways, the contents of this book are timely not only because of this but also because at that same time it had already been a criminal offence in England and Wales for five years. So in this book, the authors have been in the privileged position of being able to draw on the lessons from, and the debates emerging in, both of those contexts.

Sandra Walklate would particularly like to thank her friend and colleague Dr Kate Fitz-Gibbon of Monash University for the many conversations on this and other issues along with the writing we have done together and with others in making sense of, and responding to, the changing Australian policy landscape. I could not have asked for a better friend or colleague. In addition, my Australian working life with fellow academics at the Monash Gender and Family Violence Prevention Centre could not be bettered anywhere. The more the world has challenged us, the closer a working unit we have become: a major testimony to both them and to the environment of Monash University in which we have flourished.

Working with Charlotte has been a joy. We began academic life as PhD supervisor and PhD student but have since moved well beyond this, embarking on writing and research projects together. Charlotte's enthusiasm and positive spirit is infectious and importantly makes work fun! Finally but in no way last, my husband and partner Ron Wardale has ensured living and working from home since March 2020 has never been a challenge for either of us. Thank you.

Charlotte Barlow would like to extend her sincerest gratitude to Sandra, who has been the most fantastic mentor, colleague, and friend. Sandra is a juggernaut in the field, yet remains to be so generous with her time, committed to supporting colleagues, particularly early career researchers, and is the best critical friend. I will be forever grateful that you allowed me to continue badgering to work with you post-PhD!

Finally, Charlotte would like to thank her family. Nancy, for many people, 2020 was understandably a very dark year, but because of you, it was the best for us. You fill our world with joy every day. To Johnny, my husband and biggest supporter, thank you for everything. To Alfie, the silliest and most loveable dog. And to my Mum, Dad, Gemma, Matt, Elanor, and Annie – I love you all.

1   What is 'coercive control'?

Introduction

Coercive control has been recognized as a feature of intimate partner relationships since the early 1980s. The term was first used by Schechter (1982) and has been differently emphasized in the work of Johnson (1995) and Stark (2007) among others since. More recently, the invidious effects of its presence in intimate partner relationships has been documented in relation to children (Callaghan et al., 2018), on mothering practices (Heward-Belle, 2017), on what Elizabeth (2017) has called 'custody stalking', as well as in the digital world (Harris and Woodlock, 2019). The purpose of this introduction is to document the history and development of this concept, paying particular attention to its diverse and contested usage. This overview will set the scene for the chapters that follow, each of which will pick up on and examine the utility of this concept as a way of understanding criminal behaviour, experiences of victimization, and the kinds of policy responses that have been developed in light of this knowledge. However, first a brief consideration of what is meant by coercive control.

Coercive control: a definition

ANROWS (2021: 1) states:

> Coercive control is a course of conduct aimed at dominating and controlling another (usually an intimate partner, but can be other family members) and is almost exclusively perpetrated by men against women.

The key element in this definition, and one that runs through all definitions of coercive control, is the emphasis on a course of conduct:

DOI: 10.4324/9781003019114-1

a repeated pattern of behaviour designed to undermine the autonomy of another individual. It is in essence the invidious assertion of male power, not necessarily by force and/or physical violence, but by strategies of psychological, emotional, and financial abuse. It is the way in which these strategies impact upon a woman's sense of herself that leads Stark (2007) to talk of coercive control as a liberty crime. However, as understandings of coercive control have increasingly made their presence felt in the policy domain, the question of who does what to whom and how effectively policy and practice can capture that dynamic have come under ever closer scrutiny. That scrutiny challenges the gendered assumptions outlined in the ANROWS definition above (with many men's groups arguing that they too are subjected to coercive control); the ability of practitioners to recognize who the victim and who the perpetrator might be when responding to coercive control (resulting in the problem of misrecognition, i.e., identifying the defensive strategies of a woman as constituting perpetration), and the capacity of the criminal law (recently labelled by Goodmark (2018) as the criminalization thesis) to respond to relationships characterized by coercive control. In what follows, we discuss each of these issues in turn, but first a brief overview of the historical and contextual development of this concept will set the scene for understanding its contestation.

Coercive control: a brief conceptual history

There are two features to the ongoing debate about coercive control that remain unreconciled; the extent to which it is gendered (that is something that men engage in over their female partners) and the extent to which physical violence is, or is not, a constituent element of such controlling behaviour. In some respects, these features echo the wider debate over the gendered nature and the extent of domestic abuse. This is often characterized as a methodological issue between those who favour the Conflicts Tactics Scale as their preferred measuring instrument for such abuse and those who favour more feminist informed approaches (as an example of this debate, consider the differences between the work of Straus (1979) and Dobash and Dobash (1992)). Frequently referred to as the gender-symmetrical versus the gender-asymmetrical debate, Stark (2007) observed that this was a somewhat sterile distinction to make when viewed from the position of women seeking help during the 1990s. He suggests that for them, the recourse to the criminal justice process, because of their experiences of violence, was their only route to call their abusers to account. This did not mean that this kind of physical abuse was the only kind they had been subjected to. His work, among that of many others, documents a wide range of abusive behaviours endemic in problematic relationships, from emotional abuse to psychological abuse to financial abuse, all designed to control female partners. Enter the concept of coercive control.

Schechter (1982) was one of the first scholars to name domestic abuse as a form of coercive and controlling behaviour. She conceptualized such abuse as gendered, in which predominantly men sought to gain control over women. Schechter (1982: 216) suggested that abusers used physical, sexual, emotional, financial abuse, and threats to dominate female intimate partners, and these strategies facilitated a pattern of coercive control. This work published just after Straus' (1979) introduction of the Conflicts Tactics Scale, resulted in over a decade of work, concerned to establish the extent to which such abuse was or was not gendered.

The work of Johnson (1995; 2008) in many ways sits between that of Schechter and Straus. He suggested that different types of domestic abuse existed and created a typology comprising four types of such abuse. The first type in this typology he called coercive controlling violence. He suggested that this comprised a pattern of emotionally abusive intimidation, coercion, and control coupled with physical violence against partners. In his early work, Johnson used the term *intimate terrorism* to capture this form of abuse. In many ways, his articulation of coercive controlling violence is similar to the patterned abuse presented in the Duluth Power and Control Wheel (Pence and Paymar, 1993). This wheel features various forms of abuse, such as intimidation, emotional abuse, isolation, minimizing, denying, asserting male privilege, economic abuse, coercion, and threats (Pence and Paymar, 1993). Johnson (2008) suggests that because such nonviolent control tactics are often just as effective in exerting power and control without the use of physical violence, coercive controlling violence does not necessarily manifest itself in high levels of violence. In his work, coercive controlling violence is perpetrated primarily by men. Moreover, while Johnson (2008) recognizes the ways in which patriarchy and gender inequality contribute to this kind of gender asymmetry, he does not develop this understanding to the same extent and in the same way as Stark (2007) has done.

Johnson (2008) goes on to make further distinctions between coercive controlling violence and other forms of violence that occur within intimate relationships. He suggests that situational couple violence is the most common type of physical aggression and has causes and consequences different from those of coercive controlling violence. This form of violence results from situations or arguments between partners that escalate on occasion to physical violence. Johnson's (2008) also discusses what he calls violent resistance, described elsewhere as self-defence. This attempts to capture when, predominantly women (victims), act violently towards their coercive and controlling partner to stop the violence they experience in their relationship. Finally, Johnson (2008) suggests the category of separation instigated violence. This is the kind of violence that occurs in a relationship at the point of separation. In all of this work, the gendered nature of the abusive behaviour features in different ways, as does the emphasis on the presence or absence of physical violence. However, in offering this level of nuance to understanding the complexity of abuse in interpersonal relationships, Johnson has faced criticism for minimizing the overall gendered nature of domestic abuse. Conversely, this is the key emphasis in Stark's (2007) work.

Stark's (2007) concept of coercive control has gained significant currency across the world since the publication of his book. He defines coercive control as 'calculated, malevolent conduct deployed almost exclusively by men to dominate individual women by intervening repeated physical abuse with three equally important tactics, namely intimidation, isolation and control' (Stark 2007: 2). This version of coercive control attempts to capture the 'cage' of intimidating, degrading, and regulatory practices engineered by abusers to inculcate fear and threat in victims' everyday lives (Myhill and Johnson, 2016: 357; see also Kirkwood, 1993). Stark emphasizes the centrality of gender in these processes, arguing that coercive control most frequently operates within heterosexual relationships in which men use 'social norms of masculinity and femininity... to impose their will' (2007: 6; see also Westmarland, 2015) and argues that coercive control can exist in relationships with or without the presence of physical violence. Importantly, it is the threat of violence and abuse that limits victims' autonomy, choice, and day-to-day activities. As a result, a victim's psychological well-being can be adversely affected, with the seriousness of this varying depending on factors such as the extent of control, the type of tactics used, and/or a victim's level of resilience and coping strategies (Williamson, 2010). The adverse effects of a sustained period of coercive control amount to psychological trauma and in some cases can result in suicide (Bettinson, 2020). Central to Stark's (2007) theorization of coercive control is that the abuse comprises a sustained course of conduct rather than isolated incidents of abuse.

This brief overview offers a flavour of the way in which the key proponents of this concept developed and interpreted its salience in understanding domestic abuse since the early 1980s. From this overview, it is self-evident that while there is some common agreement on the presence of coercive control, there is not the same level of agreement on the extent of its presence and/or how it might be manifested. Indeed, in a recent overview of work using this concept Hamberger et al. (2017) identified 22 different definitions and operationalizations of this concept, all of which led to different research findings on its efficacy. Further, Walby and Towers (2018: 11) argue that there is 'conceptual confusion' endemic in the use of this term. They particularly stress conceptual disagreements concerning the relationship between physical violence and nonphysical coercion, with coercive control being interpreted in public debate as focusing attention on nonphysical, psychological abuse, rather than physical violence. In light of this kind of confusion, they propose a third approach to conceptualizing domestic abuse. This they call 'domestic violent crime' (Walby and Towers, 2018). In this framework, all violence is conceived as coercive and controlling. For them, violent crime is defined by reference to both the act and the harm it causes, where what counts as physical abuse can include more than just cuts and bruises. This approach not only centres the gendered nature of domestic abuse; it also places importance on the sex of the victim, the sex of the perpetrator, the perpetrator-victim relationship, whether it includes any sexual dynamics, and potentially any gendered motivation. One important implication of this approach is that it permits the inclusion and analysis of same-sex relationships as having the potential for the same dynamics as heterosexual relationships. In other words, in separating out sex from gender, coercive control while a predominantly gendered strategy is not necessarily sexed and/or the sole preserve of heterosexual couples. However, not all commentators agree with this approach, arguing that it affords primacy to physical abuse over psychological abuse (Donovan and Barnes, 2021; Myhill and Kelly, 2021). Furthermore, Donovan and Barnes (2019) suggest that sexuality is rendered invisible in Walby and Tower's (2018) concept of domestic violent crime.

In many ways, the debate alluded to here reaches into one that stretches beyond coercive control itself and into contemporary preoccupations with the terms sex and gender and what each of these terms might mean. These are issues not of direct relevance to the discussion here. Nevertheless, the search for the operationalization of a concept that does not assume heterosexuality as the norm is important, especially in relation to devising appropriate responses to this kind of (problematic) behaviour. As will be developed below, much of the work discussed above, and the policy responses it has generated, has collectively either given primacy to the criminal law as a solution to this problem or at least assumed a role for criminal justice in devising appropriate responses. While the efficacy of the criminal law has consistently and persistently been subjected to critique as a route for accommodating and/or understanding women's experiences of violence(s) (see inter alia Smart, 1989), this focus on the law is a recurrent theme of work relating to this concept. Before going on to discuss this issue in more detail, the notion that coercive control is gendered and more specifically is predominantly a tactic deployed by men on women, as this brief historical overview alludes to, raises some deeper questions about the concept itself that are worth thinking about a little further.

Contesting coercive control

The academic and advocacy space relating to violence against women is occupied by professionals and practitioners emanating from a range of different disciplinary backgrounds and practice orientations. Such differences inevitably can result in different emphases in understanding, analysing, and applying this concept to (primarily) women's real lives. It can also result in differences in emphases on how to respond to coercive control. It is little wonder then that it is a contested concept. However, reflecting on these differences enables some deeper reflection about the concept itself. Here these issues will be considered along several dimensions: coercive control as a clinical–psychological construct, a gendered construct, a social construct, and/or a legal construct. In experiential terms of course, for someone who has been routinely subjected to such control for a considerable length of time, such separations are neither real nor meaningful. However, for analytical purposes, these dimensions offer some assistance in making sense of the debates generated by this concept. To be clear, there is no hierarchy intended or implied between the different dimensions highlighted in the discussion that follows.

Coercive control as a clinical/psychological concept

In some respects, this way of thinking about coercive control resonates most readily with the work of Stark (2007). His work is deeply embedded in advocacy and practice: listening to and providing support for women in making sense of their lives and how to rebuild them in the aftermath of an intimate relationship with an abuser. In this context, coercive control offers women a valuable and meaningful way in which to make sense of what has gone before and offers them strategies for moving on with their lives. In this sense, it can inform therapeutic practices in very powerful ways. As such, it can be understood as both a clinical concept, grounded in practice, and as a psychological concept, grounded in experience, offering a way for women to make sense of the behaviours they have been subjected to and the consequences of those behaviours on their sense of themselves as individuals with person hood. However, being grounded in experience and practice does not necessarily mean that it is a concept readily translatable into other forms of policy response. Coercive control as a clinical/psychological concept needs some work for it to make sense as a legal concept (Walklate et al., 2018). This is revisited in Chapter 4.

Coercive control as a gendered construct

In much of the work cited so far in this introduction, the assumption has been made that coercive control is predominantly deployed by men over women. Although the gendered nature of domestic abuse is well documented, there are several issues here. First, it is the case that not all men control women using tactics of this kind. Gadd et al. (2019) have asked: why [do] some men choose to secure control in coercive ways when so many other aspects of their lives appear out of control? They ask this question in relation to unravelling the complex interplay between alcohol, drugs, and mental illness that feature in the use of all kinds of violence(s) in men and women's lives, but it is a good question to reflect upon more generally. How, why, and under what conditions do some men deploy coercive and controlling tactics and others under those same conditions do not? Can only men deploy such tactics? Where do non-heteronormative relationships feature here? If social class, caste, religion, and so on were added to gender, what light would this level of complexity, which is also a part of people's everyday lives, throw upon the use and deployment of coercive control? This latter question overlaps with the next area of contestation.

Coercive control as a social construct

Thinking about coercive control as a social construct brings to the foreground the question of the contexts in which it is most likely to have resonance. Wilson (2020) and Nancarrow (2019) pointedly remind us that Indigeneity (as one of a range of social structural features of people's lives) informs how things such as family violence (to use the Australian Indigenous preferred term) can be differently experienced, understood, and responded to. In such contexts, the coercive control experienced within a relationship can be seen as preferable to the coercive control experienced by the state. This example is used here as one way of encouraging reflection on the question of whose interests and experiences does this concept capture? Does this concept resonate most readily, as a way of making sense of one's life and devising a course of action in the light of that sense-making, for the white, articulate, Northern, woman for whom autonomy is taken for granted? In other words, are there implicit groups for whom this concept works because it taps into their social position? Which are the categories of women (and others) for whom this concept does not resonate? If the recourse to law is the preferred policy response to coercive control, this question has pertinence.

Coercive control as a legal construct

As much of the preceding discussion has intimated, much activity in terms of responding to coercive control has focused on the law as an appropriate avenue for intervention. Not all jurisdictions have embarked on this embrace in the same way. Some jurisdictions have added coercive control to already existing laws, some have developed stand-alone offences of coercive control, some have created spaces for the professional voices to speak in court about the effects of coercive control, and some have sought to amend mitigating defences for murder based on the presence of coercive control. (For an overview of these different responses, see Walklate and Fitz-Gibbon, 2019). In addition, in some jurisdictions there is capacity for the recognition of coercive control in the civil as opposed to the criminal law (e.g., in the State of Victoria, Australia). Much of this activity has taken place with little recognition of the role of coercion in law more generally (Brunk, 1979) or of the law itself as a source of coercion and control (Walklate and Fitz-Gibbon, 2021). Nonetheless, these interventions have been developed and implemented largely within a wider ideological adherence to what Goodmark (2018) has called the 'criminalization thesis'. While her appreciation of the power of this thesis is largely oriented towards the United States, as legal responses to coercive control have developed across the globe, this thesis has some resonance for the concerns of this book and is developed more fully in the chapters that follow.

From this brief thematic overview, it can be seen that coercive control as a concept and a lens through which to understand women's lives and develop appropriate responses to the violence(s) they experience is subject to contestation. Perhaps what is less contested is the extent to which the version of this concept, as proposed in the work of Evan Stark (2007), has risen up the policy agenda across the globe. It is to an appreciation of the influence of that work that we now turn.

Responding to coercive control

Stark's (2007) conceptualization of coercive control is one of the main lenses through which domestic abuse is now understood. This is particularly the case in the United Kingdom. The embrace of coercive control in England and Wales first became discernible with its inclusion in the Home Office definition of domestic abuse, introduced in 2014. In 2015, this definition became embedded into legislation, with the introduction of Section 76 of the Serious Crime Act. This legislative embrace has generated interest internationally, particularly from Ireland, Denmark, and Australia, though it should be noted that Tasmania introduced two offences: one of economic abuse and another of emotional abuse and intimidation in their Family Violence Act in 2004. Both of these concerns fit within the rubric of coercive control as defined by Stark, and both are couched in terms of an ongoing course of conduct (see McMahon and McGorrery, 2016). Before going on to consider these specific legislative interventions in more detail, it will be useful to reflect upon some of the problems inherent in translating the experience of this kind of abuse into something that is actionable and doable in law.

The first problem lies in the relationship between psychological/emotional abuse and physical abuse, both of which frequently involve a pattern of behaviour and/or a course of conduct. As the discussion above has intimated, physical and psychological abuse are not mutually exclusive; neither is one the prerequisite of the other, nor do they exist in a hierarchical relationship with each other. The presence of either/both can result in a woman's life being marked by fear, intimidation, and a loss of autonomy, all of which reduce her capacity to leave an abusive situation. Taken together, they result in entrapment (Buzawa et al., 2017). Of course, part of the debate that the recognition of coercive control has generated is how and to what extent the criminal justice system is the most appropriate avenue through which to respond to such a course of conduct, when most criminal justice systems are geared up to responding to incidents rather than processes. This is discussed in more detail in Chapter 4.

The second problem arising from the translation of coercive control into a legislative policy response is its focus on women's autonomy. Leaving aside the gendered assumptions inherent in coercive control as explicated in the work of Stark and others (considered above), the presumption of female autonomy is contingent upon a wide range of social and cultural factors. Moreover, what constitutes female autonomy has been the subject of considerable debate among feminists. While individualistic and atomistic understandings of autonomy are widely rejected in favour of an understanding of such autonomy as being relational, there remain hard challenges for feminists in appreciating what autonomy might mean for women. Put simply, if a woman defers to her partner's wishes, adapts to her lot in life, and/or adheres to practices that can be considered oppressive, the question remains as to whether or not she retains autonomy. This is not the place to review the considerable feminist work that has debated each of these challenges and proposed differing responses to them. It is perhaps sufficient at this juncture to point out that how and under what conditions women might make a choice of their own (as one element of autonomy), once that woman's life is placed within the structural and cultural context in which she lives, is difficult to assert.

Interestingly, Stark's (2007) assertion of coercive control as a liberty crime reveals much about the social and cultural context of his work having been generated in the United States in which, just as one place to start, the constitution affords individuals rights. However, it is recognized that structural constraints such as ethnicity, disability, and poverty impede some women's access to such rights and associated resources. Awareness of this context and its relevance for appreciating how and under what circumstances responses to coercive control may travel to other jurisdictions is returned to later in this book. Centring the importance of autonomy as coercive control does is connected to the third problem associated with this concept discussed here. That is the relationship between autonomy and intimacy. Finding a balance between autonomy and intimacy is a challenge for any relationship (Renzetti, 1992). Leaving aside for the moment the question of cultural context raised above, charting a course between retaining autonomy, making compromises, and what issues involve reaching a compromise can be considered to be part and parcel of 'equitable' relationships, particularly in Northern, twenty-first century understandings of being in a relationship. If this is how relationships are seen to work, the question that arises for the concept of coercive control is, 'When does compromise equate with control'?

Crossman and Hardesty (2018) have endeavoured to explore this question empirically. In their work, they make a distinction between women's experiences of constraint through commitment and constraint through force. They interviewed 22 divorced women and from that retrospective data found that control was a feature of all these women's relationships but that this control was manifested in different ways. For some women, control/constraint was felt and experienced as a constituent element of compromises they made because of their commitment to the relationship, many of which could be seen as part of the social expectations permeating their lives. However, for those women who experienced control/ constraint through force, the compromises made might have been the same, but the emphasis was different. For these women, the men in their lives *used* social norms and expectations to constrain them. Interestingly, both groups experienced the use of physical violence, but their experience of control (as either through compromise or force) was not related to this violence. Work of this kind, rooted in listening to women's experiences, offers a much more nuanced understanding of how and when coercive control might equate with entrapment. Importantly, they imply that control may not always be coercive.

So here again, when considering how to respond to coercive control, practitioners and policy makers are faced with the question of when does a 'normal' intimate relationship become problematic, when the actual behaviours engaged in are the same? Fear is often understood as a key indicator, but the all-consuming nature of controlling behaviour means that it is often difficult for victim/survivors to articulate what specific behaviours led them to feel afraid or trapped. In summary, there are blurred boundaries between romance, intimacy, and coercive control (Chung, 2005) all of which may change over time. In other words, what was once non-problematic may become problematic. Again, awareness of this kind of nuance poses tricky questions for devising appropriate policy responses, particularly when those policy responses might result in control by the state as a consequence (Walklate and Fitz-Gibbon, 2021).

Despite these problems, efforts have been, and continue to be made, to create legislation that criminalizes coercive control. It will be of value to take a closer look at the definition of coercive control as found in an example of this kind of legislation, here drawing on the Domestic Abuse Act (2021) relevant to England and Wales. This legislation puts a definition of domestic abuse on a statutory basis for this first time and states:

> Behaviour of a person ('A') towards another person ('B') is 'domestic abuse' if—
> A and B are each aged 16 or over and are personally connected to each other, and the behaviour is abusive.
> Behaviour is 'abusive' if it consists of any of the following—
>
> physical or sexual abuse;
> violent or threatening behaviour;
> controlling or coercive behaviour;

economic abuse (see subsection (4));

psychological, emotional or other abuse;

and it does not matter whether the behaviour consists of a single incident or a course of conduct.

'Economic abuse' means any behaviour that has a substantial adverse effect on B's ability to—acquire, use or maintain money or other property, or obtain goods or services.

The legislation defines 'personally connected' in the following way:

For the purposes of this Act, two people are 'personally connected' to each other in any of the following applies—

they are, or have been, married to each other;

they are, or have been, civil partners of each other;

they have agreed to marry one another (whether or not the agreement has been terminated);

they have entered into a civil partnership agreement (whether or not the agreement has been terminated);

they are, or have been, in an intimate personal relationship with each other;

they each have, or there has been a time when they each have had, a parental relationship in relation to the same child (see subsection (2));

they are relatives.

(Domestic Abuse Act, 2021, Chapter 17, part 1)

While the Home Office (2015: 3) suggested that the then introduction of the offence of coercive and controlling behaviour 'closes a gap' in law, since the existing stalking and harassment offences as defined in law could not be applied to ongoing intimate relationships, the 2021 legislation supersedes this position. Clearly, the 2021 legislation is extensive in both what it includes as domestic abuse and who can commit such abuse. For this first time, it recognizes people as personally connected even though they may have left the relationship. However, while this legislation, and the 2015 legislation, draws heavily on the work of Evan Stark, there are some notable differences when compared to his work. For example, unlike the legislation introduced in Scotland in 2018, the legislation in England and Wales is gender-neutral and allows for the possibility of other family relationships to be included within its terms (Stark and Hester, 2019; Burman and Brooks-Hay, 2018).

The 2015 legislation was hailed as a move forward in recognizing the persistent nature of domestic abuse and in setting a framework for encouraging criminal justice professionals to embrace such abuse as a process occurring over time rather than as a one-off event. This emphasis has been maintained in the 2021 Act. The 2015 legislation did not cover coercive control occurring outside an ongoing relationship, or where the connected parties did not live together. This was contrary to extensive evidence that identifies coercive control as a significant issue in intimate relationships during and post separation (Dekeseredy et al., 2017). This has clearly been recognized in the 2021 Act. However, the ongoing failure to recognize coercive control as being a form of gender-based violence overwhelmingly perpetrated by men and experienced by women persists. While this dilutes the core, evidence-based premise of coercive control as conceptualized by Stark (2007), it is an ongoing area of contestation with UK-based organizations like Mankind being at the forefront of these debates. The jury is still out on not whether some women engage in coercive and controlling behaviours: available empirical evidence and specific cases taken to court relating to female offenders of coercive control stand as testimony to the fact that they do. However, what remains uncertain is the nature and impact of such behaviours on men when compared with women and/or any other sex/gender categories. This issue is taken up more fully in Chapter 3. One final observation concerning the UK legislation is that the concept of coercive control has been extended to include family members. Arguably, this again undermines the evidence-based premise of what coercive control is, that is, a form of abuse that takes place primarily in ongoing or previous intimate partner relationships (Stark, 2007; Kelly and Westmarland, 2016). The extent to which the concept of coercive control has become increasingly elastic as it has entered public and policy discourse is revisited in the conclusion to this book.

As suggested above, the Scottish legislation defined coercive control somewhat differently. The Scottish definition embraces the gendered nature of coercive control and is narrower in focus than that of England and Wales, focusing on behaviours between partners and ex-partners rather than including other family members. As Burman and Brooks-Hay (2018) point out, there are other differences too:

> the Scottish offence requires proof of a 'course of behaviour' involving abuse on at least two occasions (so single incidents are not covered, but would be by other existing laws). Additionally, for an offence of domestic abuse to have been committed, two other conditions must be met: the behaviour needs to be such that a reasonable person would consider it likely to cause the victim physical

or psychological harm; and that the accused either intended to cause the victim physical or psychological harm, or else has been reckless as to the causing of such harm. Hence, the focus is on the behaviour of the alleged perpetrator rather than the victim's reaction or the evidencing of actual harm to them.

(ibid: 74)

Differences such as these obviously matter when it comes to implementation and subsequent intervention comparisons when looking for evidence of efficacy. These issues are discussed in more detail in Chapter 4. However, because of the gendered emphasis in the Scottish law and the explicit engagement of feminist informed advocacy organizations in the consultation process and development of this law (Scott, 2020), the Scottish response has been celebrated as the 'gold standard' in this arena (Stark, 2020). Its status as the gold standard is evidenced in the extent to which this response is being cited in ongoing debates concerning the need to criminalize coercive control in different states in Australia.

The contemporary debate concerning coercive control in Australia provides an interesting case in point on the nature, extent, and influence of Stark's (2007) work; the powerful and highly emotive impact of high-profile, widely publicized, and tragic incidents of intimate partner homicide in Australia where coercive control was present; and the voices of particular advocates of criminalization, like that of investigative journalist Jess Hill, whose book *See what you made me do* published in 2019, has had considerable impact. The specificities of this debate need not be of concern at this juncture, except to say that the difficulties of transferring a legal response informed by a concept developed in one jurisdiction and applying that same response elsewhere in the globe are both neatly overlooked and elided in this debate. At the same time, ANROWS (the Australian organization devoted to evidencing women and children's experiences of violence and informing policy responses) has pointed to three policy concerns about the moves to criminalize coercive control in Australia. That organization has pointed out that before criminalization makes sense, there is a need to harmonize definitions of family violence across the states of Australia, a need to build a robust evidence base on the impact of criminalization, and finally a need for a whole system culture change on family violence. The nuances of the criminalization debate are discussed in much greater detail in Chapter 4.

The purpose of this book

From these introductory comments, it is possible to discern that the debates concerning coercive control, who does what to whom, and the possibilities for translating these considerations into policy and practice is a fast-moving context. This book aims to offer a critical appreciation of these developments and the problems and possibilities associated with them becoming embedded in law and criminal justice practice. In this book, we consider coercion and coercive control as it features in both offending and victimization noting the importance of understanding the nature of coercion more generally as the backcloth against which to understand coercive control. This discussion endeavours to recognize the nature of people's real lives and the extent to which coercive control, particularly its translation to criminal law, resonates with those lives. In doing so, the book is divided into five further chapters. Chapter 2 considers the role of coercion/coercive control as they might frame understandings of pathways into crime and/or as a defence for criminal behaviour. The case of Sally Challen is considered in this chapter alongside the developments that have followed since the ruling in that case. This chapter discusses the longer history of how coercion has featured in law and the problems and possibilities of coercive control as a specific defence considering this history. Chapter 3 considers coercive control as a strategy of victimization and documents its efficacy as a way of making sense of the nature and impact of coercive control in relation to violence against women more generally. This chapter will consider in more detail the case for and against understanding coercive control as gendered and will develop further an appreciation of the experiences that are included and excluded in this debate. This chapter situates these considerations against an appreciation of what might constitute a 'normal' relationship posing the questions: when does coercion become controlling and, consequently, when and under what circumstances does coercive control translate to people's real lives? Chapter 4 considers the issues emerging from the increasing presence of the push to criminalize coercive control. This chapter situates these pressures within the increasing presence of critical voices in relation to criminalization in this field more generally and not only considers the specific problems of criminalization itself (for whom might this work, which groups might be included and excluded by it), but also raises the more fundamental questions concerning women's agency and the role of the state. The last substantive chapter reflects more deeply on the criminalization turn present in the policy coercive control creep and places these considerations within neoliberalism, the culture of control, and carceral feminism. Within these developments, the argument will be made that women's voices have been co-opted in the interests of the furtherance of the (neo-liberal) state, and this chapter will reflect on the consequences of these developments and for whom. Finally, the concluding chapter will consider how and under what conditions coercive control is a useful concept for making sense of and responding to violence against women, offering a word of caution against its wholesale embrace as constituting a step forward for either women or criminal justice.

References

Australia's National Research Organisation for Women's Safety. (2021). *Defining and responding to coercive control: Policy brief* (ANROWS Insights, 01/2021). Sydney: ANROWS.

Bettinson V (2020) A comparative evaluation of offences: Criminalising abusive behaviour in England, Wales, Scotland, Ireland and Tasmania. In McMahon M and McGorrery P (Eds.), *Criminalising coercive control: Family violence and the criminal law* (pp. 197–217). Singapore: Springer.

Brunk GG (1979) The problem of voluntariness and coercion in the negotiated plea. *Law and Society Review 13*(2): 527–553. https://doi.org/10.2307/3053267

Burman M and Brooks-Hay O (2018) Aligning policy and law? The creation of a domestic abuse offence incorporating coercive control. *Criminology and Criminal Justice 18*(1): 67–83. https://doi.org/10.1177%2F1748895817752223

Buzawa ES, Buzawa CG and Stark E (2017) *Responding to domestic violence: The integration of criminal justice and human services* (5th ed.). Thousand Oaks, CA: SAGE publications.

Callaghan JEM, Alexander JH, Sixsmith J and Fellin LC (2018) Beyond 'witnessing': Children's experiences of coercive control in domestic violence and abuse. *Journal of Interpersonal Violence 33*(10): 1551–1581. https://doi.org/10.1177%2F0886260515618946

Chung D (2005) Violence, control, romance and gender equality: Young women and heterosexual relationships. *Women's Studies International Forum 28*(6): 445–455. https://psycnet.apa.org/doi/10.1016/j.wsif.2005.09.005

Crossman K and Hardesty J (2018) Placing coercive control at the center: What are the processes of coercive control and what makes control coercive? *Psychology of Violence 8*(2): 196–206. https://psycnet.apa.org/doi/10.1037/vio0000094

DeKeseredy WS, Dragiewicz M, and Schwartz MD (2017) *Abusive endings: Separation and divorce violence against women.* Oakland, CA: University of California Press.

Dobash R and Dobash R (1992) *Women, violence and social change.* London: Routledge.

Domestic Abuse Act (2021) https://www.gov.uk/government/publications/domestic-abuse-bill-2020-factsheets/domestic-abuse-bill-2020-overarching-factsheet

Donovan C and Barnes R (2021) Re-tangling the concept of coercive control: A view from the margins and a response to Walby and Towers (2018). *Criminology and Criminal Justice 21*(2): 242–257. https://doi.org/10.1177/1748895819864622

Elizabeth V (2017) Custody stalking: A mechanism of coercively controlling mothers following separation. *Feminist Legal Studies 25*(2): 185–201. https://doi.org/10.1007/s10691-017-9349-9

Gadd D, Henderson J, Radcliffe P, Stephens-Lewis D, Johnson A and Gilchrist G (2019) The dynamics of domestic abuse and drug and alcohol dependency. *British Journal of Criminology 59*(5): 1035–1053. https://doi.org/10.1093/bjc/azz011

Goodmark L (2018) *Decriminalizing domestic violence: A balanced policy approach to intimate partner violence.* Oakland, CA: University of California Press.

Hamberger K, Larsen SE and Lehrner A (2017) Coercive control in intimate partner violence. *Aggression and Violent Behavior 37*: 1–11. https://psycnet.apa.org/doi/10.1016/j.avb.2017.08.003

Harris B and Woodlock D (2019) Digital coercive control: Insights from two landmark domestic violence studies. *The British Journal of Criminology 59*(3): 530–550. https://doi.org/10.1093/bjc/azy052

Heward-Belle S (2017) Exploiting the 'good mother' as a tactic of coercive control: Domestically violent men's assaults on women as mothers. *Journal of Women and Social Work 32*(3): 374–389. https://doi.org/10.1177%2F0886109917706935

Home Office (2015) https://www.legislation.gov.uk/ukpga/2015/9/section/76/enacted

Johnson MP (1995) Patriarchal terrorism and common couple violence: Two forms of violence against women. *Journal of Marriage and the Family 57*(2): 283–294. https://psycnet.apa.org/doi/10.2307/353683

Johnson MP (2008) *A typology of domestic violence: Intimate terrorism, violent resistance, and situational couple violence.* Lebanon, NH: University Press of New England.

Kelly L and Westmarland N (2016) Naming and defining 'domestic violence': lessons from research with violent men. *Feminist Review 112*(1): 113–127. http://doi.org/10.1057/fr.2015.52

Kirkwood C (1993) *Leaving abusive partners.* London: Sage.

McMahon M and McGorrery P (2016) Criminalising emotional abuse, intimidation and economic abuse in the context of family violence: The Tasmanian experience. *University of Tasmania Law Review 35*(2): 1–22.

Myhill A and Johnson K (2016) Police use of discretion in response to domestic violence. *Criminology and Criminal Justice 16*(1): 3–20. http://doi.org/10.1177/1748895815590202

Myhill A and Kelly L (2021) 'Counting with understanding? What is at stake in debates on researching domestic violence'. *Criminology and Criminal Justice 21*(3): 280–296. https://doi.org/10.1177/1748895819863098

Nancarrow H (2019) *Unintended consequences of domestic violence law: Gendered aspirations and racialised realities.* Hampshire: Palgrave MacMillan.

Pence E and Paymar M (1993) *Education groups for men who batter: The Duluth model.* New York: Springer. https://doi.org/10.1891/9780826179913

Renzetti C (1992) *Violent betrayal: Partner abuse in lesbian relationships.* Newbury Park, CA: Sage.

Schechter S (1982) *Women and male violence: The visions and struggles of the Battered Women's Movement.* Cambridge, MA: South End Press.

Scott M (2020) The making of the new 'gold standard': The Domestic Abuse (Scotland) Act 2018. In McMahon M and McGorrery P (Eds.), *Criminalising coercive control: Family violence and the criminal law* (pp. 176–194). Singapore: Springer.

Smart C (1989) *Feminism and the power of law.* London: Routledge.

Stark E (2007) *Coercive control: How men entrap women in personal life.* Oxford: Oxford University Press.

Stark E and Hester M (2019) Coercive control: Update and review. *Violence against Women* 25(1): 81–104. https://doi.org/10.1177%2F1077801218816191

Stark E (2020) The 'coercive control framework': Making law work for women. In McMahon M and McGorrery P (Eds.), *Criminalising coercive control: Family violence and the criminal law* (pp. 33–49). Singapore: Springer.

Straus M (1979) 'Measuring intrafamily conflict and violence: The Conflict Tactics (CT) scales'. *Journal of Marriage and the Family 41*: 75–88.

Walby S and Towers J (2018) Untangling the concept of coercive control: Theorizing domestic violent crime. *Criminology and Criminal Justice 18*(1): 7–28. https://doi.org/10.1177%2F1748895817743541

Walklate S and Fitz-Gibbon K (2019) The criminalisation of coercive control: The power of law? *International Journal for Crime, Justice and Social Democracy 8*(4): 94–108. https://doi.org/10.5204/ijcjsd.v8i4.1205

Walklate S, Fitz-Gibbon K and McCulloch J (2018) Is more law the answer? Seeking justice for victims of intimate partner violence through the reform of legal categories. *Criminology and Criminal Justice 18*(1): 115–121. https://doi.org/10.1177%2F1748895817728561

Walklate S and Fitz-Gibbon K (2021) Why criminalise coercive control? The complicity of the criminal law in punishing women through furthering the power of the state. *International Journal for Crime, Justice and Social Democracy 9*(4). https://doi.org/10.5204/ijcjsd.1829

Westmarland N (2015) (Ed.) *Violence against women: Criminological perspectives on men's violences.* London: Routledge.

Williamson E (2010) Living in the world of the domestic violence perpetrator: Negotiating the unreality of coercive control. *Violence against Women 16*(12): 1412–1423. https://doi.org/10.1177%2F1077801210389162

Wilson D (2020) *Colonisation, race and coercive control.* Paper presented at Criminalizing Coercive Control Webinar, de Montford University, 30–31 July 2020.

2 Coercion into crime
The role of coercive control

Introduction

Although much of the literature related to coercion and intimate partner abuse has focussed on experiences of victimization, coercive control does not exist solely within that vacuum: it can also inform understandings of pathways into criminal behaviour. In the UK, recent attention has focussed on the case of Sally Challen and the efforts to invoke coercive control as a defence for the murder she committed against her husband prior to the introduction of coercive control as a category of offensive behaviour in 2015. Sally Challen was convicted of murdering her husband in 2011 and was sentenced to 22 years imprisonment. This was reduced to 18 years on appeal. In February 2019, three judges of the England and Wales appeal court quashed her conviction, and in June of the same year, it was ruled that Challen would not be subject to a retrial. The appeal decision was made based on new evidence provided by a psychiatrist. Informed by this evidence, the ruling states that she was suffering from two mental disorders at the time of her killing. The prosecution suggested that she was a jealous wife who 'snapped' after learning that her husband had an affair. However, her defence teams argued that her husband had bullied and belittled her throughout their marriage, controlled their finances, determined who she could be friends with, and dictated that she was not allowed to socialize without him. Her defence team and the media coverage associated with the case focussed on the coercive and controlling behaviour legislation (Section 76 Serious Crime Act 2015) when appealing her conviction, suggesting that she murdered her husband due to the extensive control and abuse she experienced throughout their marriage. However, the extent to which coercive control arguments gained traction in court is questionable and shall be discussed further later in the chapter.

DOI: 10.4324/9781003019114-2

The court ruling was heralded as a landmark case and victory by many women's rights advocates and proponents of the criminalization of coercive control, but as the judge made clear, this was a misreading of the judgement made. For the purpose of the discussion here, however, this case brings into sharp focus the extent to which coercion as a feature of both offending and co-offending behaviour has a much longer history in law, policy, and academic debate. This chapter will provide an overview of this context and, to do so, is split into five parts. The first part will briefly consider the pathways into crime literature, which has been informed by feminism. The second part will explore the ways in which coercion, informed by this feminist work, has been used to understand women's offending in a criminal justice context. The third part will consider the ways in which coercion has featured in law, both civil and criminal. The fourth part will consider the ways in which coercion has featured as a defence in criminal law. In conclusion, this chapter will consider the efficacy or otherwise of endeavouring to separate coercive control from coercion more generally.

Coercion as a pathway into crime

From the 1970s onwards, particularly in the United States, pathways literature, informed by feminist research, sought to explain how, and why, women become involved in the criminal justice system (Belknap and Holsinger, 2006; Chesney-Lind and Pasko, 2004; Daly, 1994; Richie, 1996). This research produced compelling narratives of women offenders' experiences and identified key issues and risks that often characterize women's pathways into crime and criminalization. These narratives included the impacts of childhood victimization, extreme marginalization through education and employment issues, mental health and substance misuse, and the impact of relationships, particularly with abusive male intimate partners (Daly, 1994; Richie, 1996). A smaller body of work also explored women's co-offending (with a male partner) as part of this pathways approach. This work suggests that women often engage in more serious offending with a male partner than they do when they offend alone (Koons-Witt and Schram, 2003; Mullins and Wright, 2003) and they are more likely to engage in 'gender atypical offences', such as robbery or murder, when they co-offend with a man (Becker and McCorkel, 2011). Some of this work has also focussed specifically on the experiences of women who are in an intimate relationship with their male co-offender. It is this work that has particularly influenced discussions around the possibility of women being coerced into crime by an intimate partner.

Welle and Falkin (2000) have suggested that such women often experience 'relationship policing'. This involves many aspects of their relationship and life, including participation in criminal activity, being controlled by their romantic partner/co-offender. Notably Richie (1996: 133) has argued that an intersection of gender and racial inequality can lead women to be 'compelled' into a variety of criminal behaviours, with the notion of gender entrapment helping to 'show how some women are forced or coerced into crime by their culturally expected gender roles, the violence in their intimate relationships and their social position in broader society'. The experiences of co-offending women implicated in joint enterprise cases (usually with a male intimate partner) have been detailed for the first time in a recent report by Clarke and Chadwick (2020). The research found that 90% of the women convicted of serious violence had not engaged in any violence themselves. However, many of the women in the study had experienced domestic abuse in childhood or adulthood, and almost half were experiencing domestic abuse at the time of their offence. In 87% of these cases, the co-defendant was the perpetrator of this abuse (Clarke and Chadwick 2020). Similar issues have been identified for women who are implicated in cases of serious violence with their abusive partner (Hulley, 2021). These findings point to the possible constraints that these women faced in their decisions to be involved in the offence.

In previous work, Barlow (2016) developed the concept of the 'continuum of coercion' to explain how an abusive, intimate relationship with a male partner may influence a woman's pathway into crime. This work emphasizes that a range of behaviours should be viewed as being potentially coercive in the context of co-offending, including force, threats, abuse (including physical, psychological, economic, and/ or emotional), manipulation (including love), and/ or control. A central aspect of the continuum of coercion is that such behaviours are not separate or separable from each other, but rather constitute a continuous pattern of coercive techniques. This work also highlights the ways in which experiences of offending and victimization often overlap for women and constitute important considerations when developing conceptualizations of coercion in law. In later work, Barlow and Weare (2018) highlighted the ways in which additional factors, such as substance misuse and economic deprivation, intersect with experiences of coercion into crime to produce multiple, overlapping offending motivations for women co-offenders.

Thus, the concept of coercion has a long-standing history in feminist academic literature, not just within the context of victimization. Although coercion was not explicitly discussed in this context until the 1990s, the influence of a relationship with a male, abusive partner on women's offending has long been recognized, with this infiltrating policy particularly in the UK and United States more recently. However, this is often separated from broader understandings of coercion, control, and victimization (as articulated in Section 76 of the Serious Crime Act, 2015), reflecting siloed thinking despite the commonalities between them. In the next section of this chapter, this policy context is considered in more detail, paying particular attention to the UK, with some reference to the United States.

Embedding coercion into criminal justice policy and practice

In the United States, the notion of coercion into crime has to some extent been recognized on the policy agenda since the late 1980s mostly because of the influence of the Duluth model embedded within Domestic Abuse Intervention Programs (DAIP). The Duluth model is the most commonly used perpetrator intervention programme in the United States and Canada for men who are court sanctioned to treatment for a conviction of a domestic abuse–related offence (Corvo et al., 2009). This model is rooted in feminist and sociocultural concepts of domination and control, where intimate partner abuse is used as a means by which men exhibit power and establish control over female partners (Pence and Paymar, 1993). The prominent tool within the Duluth model is the Duluth Power and Control Wheel. This details how men use male privilege, emotional and economic abuse, violence, intimidation, and isolation to control women. One section of this wheel focuses on outlining female experiences of coercion and threats. Example behaviours listed in this section include making and/or carrying out threats to do something to hurt her, threatening to leave or commit suicide, making her drop charges, or making her do illegal things. The inclusion of the latter constitutes one of the first international practice-based recognitions that coercion into crime may be a common experience for women within the wider context of intimate partner abuse.

However, the Duluth model has faced considerable criticism. For example, Stover et al. (2009) argue that there is limited evidence to suggest that Duluth programmes reduce perpetrators' levels of violence. Furthermore, critics question the science behind the programme and associated tools, as the creators are not qualified professionals and the standard of delivery has been seen to be problematic (Pender, 2012; Bohall et al., 2016). However, despite such critique, the inclusion of coercion as a method of forcing women to engage in criminal activity was an important contribution to practice-based knowledge in this area.

In the UK, the ways in which coercive, violent relationships may influence women's offending has received increasing policy attention mostly because of the work and campaigning of Baroness Corston. The Corston Report (2007) provided a review of women's experiences within the criminal justice system and offered extensive recommendations on how these could be improved. The report documents various common experiences faced by such women, including substance abuse, mental health problems, histories of violence, and abuse and harmful experiences of prison. An overarching recommendation from Corston's work was the need to adopt holistic, women centred approaches to justice. The extent to which these recommendations have been implemented and the various barriers faced have been documented elsewhere (Barr, 2018; Gelsthorpe and Russel, 2018).

Of particular significance for this chapter is Corston's (2007: 3) acknowledgment that 'coercion by men can form a route into criminal activity for some women'. She subsequently recommended that 'every agency within the criminal justice system must prioritize preparations to implement gender equality and radically transform the ways they deliver services for women' (ibid: 4). This would include an understanding of the ways in which a relationship with an abusive partner can influence women's offending. The inclusion of coercion in this report was highly significant. It was the first occasion in a UK context that coercion had been referenced in a document that had the potential to influence policy within the context of women's offending. However, the extent to which understandings of coercion into crime were explicitly and subsequently embedded into policy and practice is questionable. For example, although women-centred programmes, such as Tomorrow's Women, recognized the influence of violent relationships on women's offending in the support provision they provided, the emphasis remained on how women themselves could make positive lifestyle changes, including leaving the abuser. Such approaches have, perhaps unintentionally, responsibilized women and lead to questions concerning the extent to which such approaches are truly women centred.

A similar emphasis is echoed in the current UK government's proposed Female Offender Strategy (2019: 14). This states,

We recognise the major part that domestic abuse can play in female offending. This abuse can take different forms, including coercive and controlling behaviour. Being a victim of domestic abuse is a predictor of violent reoffending among women.

Recognizing the influence of intimate partner abuse and coercive control on women's offending is important and highlights a significant step forward in understanding the overlaps between women's victimization and offending. However, acknowledging experiences of coercive control, as conceptualized by Stark (2007), is markedly different from explicitly recognizing and providing appropriate support to women who suggest they have been coerced into crime. The nuances involved in being coerced into crime are not separate or separable from coercive control and arguably require some different thinking in relation to their practice implications. In some ways, being coerced into crime could simply be viewed as another coercive technique that perpetrators use to gain control in a relationship. However, such women cannot be readily conceptualized as a 'victim', particularly in the 'ideal' sense (Christie, 1986). It is important to consider how their 'victim-status' may influence their own understandings of the abuse they have experienced, their consequent identity formation, and the support provision they are provided with either formally by services or informally by friends, family, and community. Coerced women are likely to fall on the wrong side of 'deserving' and 'undeserving' victim narratives. Some of this nuance is lost by solely focusing policy and practice on Stark's (2007) victimization-centred conceptualization of coercive control. How issues such as these translate in law, particularly as a defence for criminal behaviour, raises additional issues.

The presence of coercion in law

Coercion has existed in law for some time. Himma (2020) explores coercion in its legal articulation and suggests that these legal features have both a descriptive and 'thick' usage. The descriptive usage describes a directive or act that can be reasonably contrived to deter non-complying behaviour without the necessity of a moral judgement attached to this. The thick element is that the threat for non-compliance is morally problematic. Himma (2020) provides an example of both elements. An armed robber threatens to kill an individual if he/she does not surrender their money. The robbers' demand for money is coercive in the descriptive sense, backed up by the thick element of the threat to kill. In an intimate partner context, a male partner could demand a woman take out a bank loan in her name on his behalf (descriptive) and threaten to kill her if she did not comply (thick). The aim of a coercive act is thus to increase the probability that in Himma's (2020) terms, a 'rational subject' would comply; therefore, the threat should not be regarded with indifference. Such conceptions of coercion dominate legal thought. However, an emphasis on rationality in relation to coercive decision-making is inherently problematic in relation to gendered experiences of intimate partner abuse. In the robber example provided by Himma (2020), the individual was not known to the victim and thus there would not be the same emotions and loyalties attached to this relationship. This is in stark contrast to coercive acts that exist within intimate relationships. Furthermore, many of the examples cited in Himma's work document isolated incidents of coercive behaviour. Yet it is known that many coercive acts occur over and through time between the same individuals, and potentially varying in severity. The question remains as to how these circumstances translate into rational, legal understandings of coercion.

Coercion has a historical presence in civil law. One notable example is in children's contact arrangements following separation and any associated child custody battles. Children are often weaponized in such contexts (Meyer, 2012), with women regularly being accused of promoting 'parental alienation'. Such accusations are often used by perpetrators of domestic abuse as reasons for continued child contact, arguing that the mother is manipulating the child/children against the father. Parental alienation (Gardner, 1992) is a contested concept, and some have argued that it is rooted in sexist assumptions about motherhood and women (Clemente and Padilla-Racero, 2015). Such issues notwithstanding, there is extensive evidence supporting child contact as a significant site for post-separation abuse and coercion (Morrison, 2015). At the same time, within the family courts, the emphasis is on maintaining contact between fathers and their children irrespective of histories of domestic abuse and often despite children's and mothers' wishes. Thus, with the complicity of the family law system, continuing contact with children can override other considerations and allows abuse to continue. Thus, in family law, circumscribed understandings of coercion, control, and its effects frequently have unintended consequences, particularly for women.

In criminal law, there are ongoing debates in relation to coercion in laws relating to rape and sexual assault. Coercion is included in the England and Wales definition of sexual assault where it states:

> sexual assault is when a person is coerced or physically forced against their will, or when a person, male or female, touches another person sexually without their consent.
>
> (CPS, 2021)

A further example of the ways in which coercion features in criminal law is in relation to forced marriage. In England and Wales, forced marriage was initially included in the civil law, under the Forced Marriage (Civil Protection) Act, which received Royal Assent as part of 4A of the Family Law Act 1996 and was subsequently implemented in England and Wales in 2008. This meant that courts were able to issue civil orders to prevent forced marriage. Criticized by various women's groups for the failure to criminalize this, the 2014 Coalition government developed a new offence relating to forced marriage under section 120/121 of the Anti-Social Behaviour, Crime and Policing Act 2014. However, since its criminalization, there have been very few convictions for forced marriage, leading to questions regarding the effective operationalization and efficacy of it (Sundari & Gill, 2009).

Brunk's (1979) work considers the coercive role of the law itself, focussing on plea bargaining and the use of coercive tactics by legal practitioners on defendants. The salience of his work highlights what the law might understand as choice. The context in which choices are made is developed more fully in Chapter 4. As Hanna (2009: 1468) suggests, 'the law forces the question of illegal coercion into a yes or no answer. The line between free choice and coercion gets drawn some-where – and you are either coerced or not'. Arguably, this captures the nature of the legal contest invoked by coercive control. These issues become especially pertinent when considering coercion as a defence for criminal behaviour.

Coercion as a defence for crime

There are three ways in which coercion either has been used as a defence in law or has been cited by barristers in mitigation for a crime; namely, Marital Coercion, Duress, and Battered Woman's Syndrome. Each of these will now be discussed in turn, in particular focussing on the extent to which they are able to capture the experiences of women who have been coerced into crime by an abusive intimate partner.

Battered woman syndrome (BWS) is recognized by the World Health Organization as a subcategory of post-traumatic stress disorder (PTSD). Although it has been used as a defence to murder in the United States, it is not a recognized defence in the UK. It involves symptoms of depression resulting from persistent domestic abuse, resulting in extreme fear and co-dependency on the abuser. According to Walker (1980), the nature of this abuse is sustained over time, therefore resulting in learned helplessness, passivity, and paralysis. Learned helplessness is crucial in both Walker's (1980) conceptualization of BWS and in the use of this as a defence. Walker (1980) suggested that learned helpless-ness helped to explain why abused women do not leave their abusers.

However, the notion that all abused women share the same psychological characteristics of learned helplessness has been extensively critiqued (Burke, 2002), and such understandings fundamentally deny women's capacity for agency, that is, the ability to make their own choices.

BWS has faced further criticism. Firstly, the inclusion of the term *battered* by implication excludes women who experience non-physical coercion and control. Arguably, a more nuanced understanding of coercion is needed to encapsulate the complex way in which a person can be coerced and the impact this can have on the well-being of the victim (Bettinson, 2019). Furthermore, although a gendered approach is important when attempting to understand experiences of coercion (Burman and Brooks-Hay, 2018), including only women's experiences, as in the defence of BWS, means that male victims' experiences or those relationships that fall outside the heterosexual model (such as same-sex relationships) are excluded (Bettinson, 2019; Dempsey, 2011). Notably, this defence is not widely used in the United States, and it is clear that this defence falls short of capturing the experiences of women who say they have been coerced by their intimate partner.

Further, Douglas, Tarrant and Tolmie (2021) suggest that BWS does not address the erroneous assumptions on the part of legal practitioners that juries will have an effective understanding of the family or domestic violence safety system and if victim-survivors accessed that system, they would be safe. As will be discussed throughout subsequent chapters, intersectional social inequity compounds women's experiences of coercive control, with the law itself often being a site of coercion. Tarrant et al. (2019) suggest that viewing intimate partner abuse as a form of social/systematic entrapment addresses some of these issues. BWS reduces the complexities of intimate partner abuse to an overly simple 'one size fits all approach'. Tarrant et al. (2019) argue that social entrapment provides a multidimensional framework, centring the ways in which structural inequality can exacerbate experiences of intimate partner abuse and undercut the safety options available to the victim-survivor. For example, in the case of Ruddelle in New Zealand, the court accepted expert evidence of social/systematic entrapment from a non-mental health professional both at trial and at sentencing. In other words, the court accepted evidence not just of coercive control but also the limitations in the safety response and the structural and intersectional inequities in the lives of Maori women. Although still convicted of Manslaughter, the case did result in a more compassionate sentence (home detention), and the judge also recognized the limits of the safety response over time for the defendant in their closing remarks. Social entrapment may therefore better capture the operation and harm of intimate partner abuse for indigenous women in particular, an argument that will be returned to in later chapters.

A defence invoking coercion that has been used in a UK context is the concept of duress. If successful, duress can result in acquittal for an individual compelled to commit an offence through fear of immediate serious physical violence. An example may be that the defendant is threatened that unless she commits a crime, she will be killed or seriously injured. If the threat is such that it overbears the defendant's ability to resist or make an informed choice, duress can be provided as a defence to any crime except for murder, attempted murder, or some forms of treason (Loveless, 2010). However, despite this technically being a defence that can be used by women who make the case that they have been coerced into crime, women are much less likely to use this defence when compared with men. Loveless (2010) suggests that the defence is likely underused by women who are coerced by an intimate partner because such abuse can easily be perceived as falling short of duress. For example, men may be more likely to experience coercion through a clearly identifiable threat of serious harm (i.e., a particular incident), rather than by sustained abuse or the 'incremental destruction of self-esteem characteristic of prolonged domestic violence' (Loveless, 2010:94).

In addition, threats of anything other than serious physical violence/loss of life are insufficient for a defence of duress rendering emotional and psychological abuse, by definition, insufficient. Dutton and Goodman (2005) suggest that the defence of duress fails to distinguish between physical force, where a victim may have no choice but to comply with demands, versus coercion, including non-physical tactics, in which a victim could choose whether or not to comply. Furthermore, to use the defence of duress, the threat of *physical* harm must be immediate. Fear of future violence is excluded, which is again problematic for women who are abused by an intimate partner. As highlighted by Loveless (2010:96),

> if continual violence has worn a woman down to a level where she has become submissive to whatever is demanded of her, she may comply with a suggestion to offend by a threat of force a few days or weeks after, even in the absence of any threat at all

This quote captures the ways in which legal understandings of coercion, as seen in the defence of duress, fail to capture both the lived experiences and contexts of coerced women's lives, thus rendering it of little value as a defence for most women. Recognition of this also foreground the inherent issues with translating a meaningful gendered conceptualization of coercion into criminal law. Feminist scholars have argued extensively that the law and legal institutions are defined by gendered discourses (Ballinger, 2000; 2012). Ballinger (2012), for example, argues that women are limited to subject positions in court due to the gendered nature of the law and its pervasive male hierarchy of knowledge. This has particularly negative consequences for female offenders who stand trial. The law is based on male experiences, and therefore women, by their very nature, fall outside the 'normal' parameters of whose experiences are included in law (Carline, 2005). Thus, even though the defence of duress is technically available to women who suggest they have been coerced into crime, by virtue of being a woman their experiences are 'othered' and excluded from legal discourse.

Marital Coercion (Section 47 of the Criminal Justice Act 1925) was a stand-alone defence before this was abolished in 2014. This stated:

> on a charge against a wife for any offence other than treason or murder it shall be a good defence to prove that the offence was committed in the presence of, and under the coercion of, the husband

This defence was abolished shortly after it was used by Vicky Pryce at her trial for perverting the course of justice in 2013, when she accepted driving license penalty points incurred by her then husband Chris Huhne in 2003. It was also used by Anne Darwin, the wife of John Darwin, the canoeist who faked his own death to claim insurance money. Anne Darwin also used the defence unsuccessfully. Similar to duress, this defence has been very rarely used by women (six occasions in total).

There were several problematic issues with this defence. Firstly, a woman had to be married to cite it, the husband had to be present at the time of the offence, and it fundamentally denied women's capacity for agency. The defence was abolished in 2014 as it was suggested that this was no longer applicable or relevant in modern society and thus outdated. However, it should be noted that there is a significant proportion of women who for social, religious, and cultural reasons cannot effectively exercise their own free will and may feel that they have to obey their partners if coerced into criminal behaviour (Barlow, 2016). Completely abolishing the defence of marital coercion means there is now no alternative comparable defence that coerced women can use. Therefore, despite defences such as marital coercion being problematic, developing defences from the standpoint of women at least attempts to account for the differences between men and women's experiences of offending and coercion.

So existing and former defences attempting to capture experiences of coercion do not adequately account for and/or reflect the experiences of women claiming to be coerced into crime by an intimate partner. Furthermore, looking beyond specific defences, the extent to which women's experiences of intimate partner abuse are recognized as a potential pathway into crime or an influencing factor on offending are rarely fully considered in mitigating circumstances. At least 63% of women in prison have experienced domestic abuse, and the implication can be made that this influenced their offending behaviour (Prison Reform Trust, 2017). The Centre for Women's Justice (CWJ) suggests that although the introduction of the coercive control offence in England and Wales recognizes the consequences of domestic abuse in intimate relationships, the criminal law still does not provide an adequate defence to those who commit offences because of such abuse. In evidence to the Domestic Abuse Act (2021), CWJ suggest that there should be a statutory defence for survivors of domestic abuse who offend, modelled on Section 45 Modern Slavery Act (2015). Despite receiving support in the House of Lords, this was rejected by the government. Thus, in England and Wales, there are still considerable gaps in the law.

Using coercive control as a criminal defence

A more recent attempt to capture coerced women's experiences in law has been to use the coercive control offence as a defence for crime. This was exemplified in the Sally Challen case, discussed in the introduction to this chapter, and has been viewed by many women's advocate groups to be a significant step forward in recognizing the experiences of abused women who kill their partners. Much of the existing debate relating to women who kill has focused on women who specifically fear physical violence following a sustained period of ongoing abuse characterized by violence or threats of violence. Bettinson (2019: 72) suggests that 'with the introduction of the offence (of coercive control), the law recognizes that the lived experiences of a domestic violence victim may centre on psychological behaviours that undermine the victim's autonomy'. As Sally Challen's case focused on her experiences of psychological, emotional, and coercive and controlling behaviours, this was perceived by many as a step forward in recognizing the web of abuse that women can experience and how this may influence their motivation for murdering their abuser. Bettinson (2019) argues that experiences of coercive control can negate moral blame and should afford a defence in the context of victims who kill their abusers. Midson (2016) suggests that a person is only criminally responsible for their *chosen* actions, which they had a fair opportunity to avoid. When applied to victims who kill their abusers, arguably this choice is eroded by coercive control (Midson, 2016; Sheehy, Stubbs and Tolmie, 2015).

However, the extent to which the Sally Challen case moved debates forward in recognizing the experiences of coerced women in law is somewhat questionable. Firstly, even though the media and Challen's defence lawyers focused on the impact of coercive control on her motivations for murdering her abuser, this did not necessarily receive the same traction in court. For example, Lady Justice Hallett said in her closing remarks:

> There might be those out there who think this (appeal) is all about coercive control but it's not... primarily it's about diagnosis of disorders that were undiagnosed at the time of the trial.
>
> (Curtis, 2019)

Thus, Challen was framed as medically and mentally unwell during her appeal, rather than her experiences of coercive control being front and centre. The successful presentation of Challen as mentally unstable fuels existing gendered scripts relating to women offenders, representing them as either 'mad' or 'bad' (Heidensohn, 1996), with Sally Challen being constructed according to the former narrative. Stark (2007) argued that rather than psychologically profiling women in court, women who kill their abusive partners are morally justified not only because of the circumstances such women face, but also because such cases are routed in a broader system of sex discrimination that deprives women of full autonomy. However, this approach clearly failed in the Challen case, though to be clear it was neither explicitly adopted. By continuing to judge women such as Challen as 'mad' abnormalizes and individualizes experiences of abuse. This process represents them as extraordinary rather than as a woman with the ordinary experiences faced by many women on a routine daily basis. It further deflects attention from the responsibility of her husband and the consequences of his abuse. In addition, being labelled as 'mad' infantalizes women in a similar way to BWS and thus denies them agency and autonomy. The Challen case has, in many ways, done less than first thought to further understandings of the ways in which evidence of coercive control can be used as a defence to better capture and respond to circumstances in which women kill their prolonged domestic abusers.

Furthermore, if coercive control was to be used more frequently as a defence for lethal violence, or if a separate stand-alone defence were to be created, there is the concern that the presence of physical violence in such cases may be increasingly linked to successful outcomes for such women (Tolmie, 2018). For example, Bettinson and Bishop (2015) point out that the judicial application of the course of conduct offending, such as stalking, frequently lapse back into an examination of individual incidents of assault since these are perceived as being easier to prove. Furthermore, Barlow et al. (2020) found that coercive control cases that featured evidence of physical violence were more likely to be police risk assessed as high risk, result in an arrest, and result in a charge in comparison with cases where no physical violence was present. If coercive control were more frequently used as a defence, or a separate defence was created, a similar hierarchy of abuse could emerge.

The Sally Challen case and most of the research in this area to date (such as that of Bettinson, 2019; Midson, 2016; Sheehy, Stubbs and Tolmie, 2015 – focus on coercively controlled women who kill their abusive partner. Translating the coercive control legislation to other offences is particularly difficult if the reliance on narratives surrounding mental ill health and 'instability', as we saw in the Sally Challen case, endures. For example, could coercive control be used as a defence if a woman shoplifted to get money for drugs on behalf of her partner? Or if she suggested she was forced to commit benefit fraud on her partner's behalf? If we take the use of coercive control as a defence in the Sally Challen case as an exemplar, it is unlikely that the same approach and reasoning would be used in such cases.

Walklate et al. (2018) suggest that, rather than using coercive control as a stand-alone defence, an alternative option to consider would be to use coercive control as a mitigating circumstance. They suggest that coercive control may be better used in expert testimony presented in court for serious offences. They similarly cite the example of women who kill their abuser; when evidence is introduced and explained by an expert practitioner, such evidence of coercive and controlling behaviour could be valuable for countering common myths (such as why didn't she leave). For example, Sheehy (2018) offers a detailed analysis of efforts in the case of Teresa Craig in Canada to invoke coercive control in support of making a case of self-defence in her trial for the murder of her partner by using the expert witness of Evan Stark himself. It was not a successful strategy in this case; however, there may well be merits in adopting this kind of approach. Citing coercive control as a mitigating circumstance for low-level offences could aid explanations of women's experiences to a jury, enabling a better understanding of the context of such cases. For such approaches to be successful, there needs to be a better understanding of coercive control and its impact on victim-survivors throughout the criminal justice system, including jurors.

However, the root of coercive control lies in gender inequalities deeply embedded in society. The work done by 'unequal power relations' (Welle and Faklin, 2000: 58) cascade through the social system. Coercive behaviours 'coalesce with normalized expectations of male and female behaviour' (Burman and Brooks-Hay, 2018: 75) and require challenging so that legal cases are judged based on 'an accurate and meaningful understanding of what is really happening in these relationships' (Hanna, 2009: 1458). The public (who sit on the jury), police, lawyers, and the judiciary may not understand the complex nuances of a relationship in which a partner enacts coercive control (Hanna, 2009). A programme of public education would be important to form the basis of more targeted training, aimed at professionals within the criminal justice system for this kind of strategy to fuel any success (see Burman and Brooks-Hay, 2018).

Can the law capture women's experiences of coercive control?

This review of coercion into crime and coercion as a defence for crime raises three difficulties in translating coercive control into law for these purposes. Firstly, both the concept (as conceived by Stark, 2007) and current responses in law fail to critically engage with the concept of agency. Stark's (2007) theory focuses explicitly on experiences of victimization. Although highly valuable (and this will be discussed at length in Chapter 3), this does not capture the experiences of women who have been coerced into crime and their capacity for agency and choice. Agency and coercion cannot be understood as being in a binary relationship of presence and absence, where the one is present only by virtue of the other's absence (Madhok et al., 2013). Coercion may exist at varying levels in coercive intimate partner relationships, as do experiences of agency and 'choice'. As Kuennen (2007) asks: where is the dividing line between coerced and voluntary decisions? Coercion is contextually dependent and exists on a continuum. Therefore, denying the presence of agency in the presence of coercion (and vice versa) does not reflect the reality of many coerced women's experiences. Acknowledging that both agency and coercion can co-exist in such relationships, albeit at differing levels, enables our understanding to move beyond notions such as 'he made me do it' and allows an exploration of how personal, social, and cultural context and other mitigating factors may impact such women's perceived offending choices and behaviour.

Importantly, it must be remembered that coerced women do ultimately engage in a 'choice' to offend. However, 'choice' as defined in law is seen as 'rational'. This fails to capture the lived realities of many women who do offend. Coerced women's 'choices' need to be situated in social context (Daly, 1994). As argued by Daly (1994: 451), cited in Comack and Brickey (2007: 27), 'it is important to acknowledge, however, that choices are never free and open, that the ability to 'choose' will be affected by broader social conditions'. Coerced women's 'choices' therefore need to be located within the context of the abuse, and the coercion and control they experience within the context of their intimate relationship. If an acknowledgement of choice was translated into legal concepts, with an understanding that this is not a free and rational choice, it would shift the focus away from the outcome of a woman's decision toward understanding the process by which she arrived at that decision. Furthermore, a common understanding of coercion, that is, forcing someone to act in a certain way, also results in dichotomous thinking (Kuennen, 2007). Yet a narrower conceptualization of coercion, one that acknowledges the choice to comply, resist, or both, even in the face of pressure, would assist a judge and other legal professionals in unravelling the complex dynamics involved in coercion generally, but particularly for coerced women.

Secondly, suggestions to translate the offence of coercive control into a defence for crime fail to account for the coercive nature of the law in and of itself. The coercive nature of the law has been extensively theorized by legal scholars and philosophers (see inter alia Lamond, 2000; Edmunson, 1995). Agents of power can exercise law and justice, which as Edmunson (1995) suggests, can be coercive. Lamond (2000) argues that the law is inherently coercive because there is provision and means by which what it says can be. The law is regularly enforced by agents such as the police, debt collectors, wheel clampers, and so on – practices that usually result in people complying with the law when they may not have done otherwise. Thus, the coercive characteristics of the law need to be constantly scrutinized. However, the extent to which women can scrutinize the law and ensure that their voices are heard is highly questionable. This is particularly the case for women already by definition marginalized from legal processes: indigenous women, disabled women, black and minority ethnic women, and women living in poverty. As previously discussed, the law is developed by men and based on men's experiences, whereby the voices of women are silenced (Ballinger, 2012; Barlow, 2016). Adding new laws and defences into a system that fundamentally fails to capture the experiences of women therefore would not go very far. Coerced women experience multiple layers of coercion: they face coercion in their relationships and by the coercive and gender-blind nature of the law itself.

Finally, coerced women often face additional structural constraints, such as economic marginalization, their indigenous status, and racism. Punitive legal responses and systematic failings by the state commonly experienced by these women also need to be considered within the broader context of coercion. The coercive nature of the law and the state more broadly can exacerbate the harms that coerced women experience. This broader structural context is important, as it is in this space that the coercive control offence was created and sanctioned. It is questionable how any defence created in this context can adequately reflect coerced women's experiences, particularly without adequate consideration of the ways in which structural inequalities contribute to their experiences of coercion, offending motivations, and criminalization.

Concluding thoughts: coercion into crime; some dilemmas

In principle, the Sally Challen case afforded the opportunity for a positive step forward in recognizing that coerced women's experiences of abuse often extend beyond physical violence. However, as discussed above, there is still some way to go in ensuring that coerced women's experiences are reflected in a meaningful way in law. In this chapter, the case has been made that those understandings of coercive control in contemporary legislative initiatives designed to take account of the motivations for some women's criminal behaviour are not, and cannot be, separate or separable from already existing or former laws with women in their sights. Importantly, the case has also been made that Stark's (2007) conceptualization of coercive control was not intended to make sense of women's criminality resulting, or not as the case may be, from their victimization. Although he mentions the possibility of using coercive control as an explanation for why women murder their abusive partner, his version of this concept does not account for women who claim that they have been coerced into crime in any significant depth. Taken together, none of these issues were considered when either developing the coercive control legislation (particularly in England and Wales) or using this concept as a defence in the Sally Challen case.

There is also a broader and well-versed question that remains unanswered. This is one that has been posed by feminist scholars for decades: are there inherent issues with the law that make it impossible to capture women's experiences? This issue is particularly relevant to coerced women, as outlined in this chapter. Despite the creation of various defences attempting to capture such women's experiences, such as duress and marital coercion in the UK, and BWS in the United States, none of them accurately represent the lives of coerced women. The ways in which mental health, instability, and unhelpful 'mad' narratives characterized the appeal case of Sally Challen suggest that developing coercive control as a defence in law and leaving the subject of law itself intact are likely to face similar issues. Nevertheless, Bettinson (2019) suggests that a specific defence of coercive control should be created to capture the harms inflicted on victims when coerced and controlled by an intimate partner. However, given the issues discussed in this chapter, questions remain as to whether such a defence would improve the experiences of coerced women who face trial or prosecution, particularly those with additional structural challenges such as ethnicity and indigenous status. Hence, we offer a word of caution in developing a new defence of coercive control since this may well result in unintended consequences.

Firstly, similar to the existing coercive control offence, cases involving physical violence may more likely lead to successful outcomes for women (Tolmie, 2018; Barlow et al., 2020). As discussed here and further in the chapters that follow, the law and criminal justice system are best equipped to deal with isolated 'incidents', as was seen with the defence of duress. The implementation issues with the coercive control legislation introduced in England and wales, discussed more fully in later chapters, would remain. On the one hand, it could be argued that even if such a defence works for just a handful of women, this is better than the current legal situation in which there is no such possibility. However, the question as to whom such a defence would most likely work and the unintended consequences for those women's experiences who are not accounted for in this way could be considerable. Secondly, offences that women commonly commit within the context of coercion, but not viewed as extreme or particularly 'serious' (such as shop-lifting or benefit fraud), may not be reflected or included in such a defence. This therefore means that while such a defence may work for some women who murder their abusive partner, for most female offenders for whom domestic abuse features as part of their pathway into crime, this would not be the case. Finally, given the issues that have come to the fore as a result of the existing coercive control legislation, it is unlikely that the complexities associated with understandings of the relationship between agency and coercion will be easily overcome. The chapters that follow will consider some of these issues further in relation to coercion as a strategy for victimization and the possibilities for criminalizing such victimization.

References

Ballinger A (2000) *Dead woman walking*. Aldershot: Ashgate.

Ballinger A (2012) A muted voice from the past: the 'silent silencing' of Ruth Ellis. *Social and Legal Studies 21*(4): 445–467.

Barlow C (2016) *Coercion and women co-offenders: A gendered pathway into crime*. Bristol: Policy Press.

Barlow C and Weare S (2018) Women as co-offenders: Pathways into crime and offending motivations. *Howard Journal of Criminal Justice 58*(1): 86–103.

Barlow C, Johnson J, Walklate S and Humphreys L (2020) Putting coercive control into practice: Problems and possibilities. *The British Journal of Criminology 60*(1): 160–179.

Barr U (2018) Gendered assisted desistance: A decade from Corston. *Safer Communities 17*(2): 81–93.

Becker S and McCorkel JA (2011) The gender of criminal opportunity: The impact of male co-offenders on women's crime. *Feminist Criminology, 6*(2): 79–110.

Belknap J and Holsinger K (2006) The gendered nature of risk factors for delinquency. *Feminist Criminology 1*(1): 48–71.

Bettinson V (2019) Aligning partial defences to murder with the offence of coercive or controlling behavior. *The Journal of Criminal Law 83*(1): 71–86.

Bettinson V and Bishop C (2015) Is the creation of a discrete offence of coercive control necessary to combat domestic violence? *Northern Ireland Legal Quarterly 66*(2): 179–197.

Bohall G, Bautista MJ and Musson S (2016) IPV and the Duluth model: An examination of the model and recommendations for future research and practice. *Journal of Family Violence 31*(8): 1029–1033.

Brunk CG (1979) The problem of voluntariness and coercion in negotiated plea bargaining. *Law and Society Review 13*(2): 527–553.

Burke AS (2002) Rational actors, self-defense, and duress: Making sense, not syndromes, out of the battered woman. *North Carolina Law Review 81*(2): 211–234.

Burman M and Brooks-Hay O (2018) Aligning policy and law? The creation of a domestic abuse offence incorporating coercive control. *Criminology & Criminal Justice 18*(1): 67–83.

Carline A (2005) Zoora Shah: An unusual woman. *Social Legal Studies*, 14 (2), 215–238.

Chesney-Lind M and Pasko L (2004) *The female offender: Girls, women and crime*. London: Routledge.

Christie N (1986) The ideal victim. In Ezzat A. Fattah (Ed.), *From crime policy to victim policy*. Basingstoke: Macmillan.

Clarke, B and Chadwick, K. (2020). *Stories of injustice: The criminalisation of women convicted under joint enterprise laws*. Manchester Metropolitan University.

Clemente M and Padilla-Racero D (2015) Are children susceptible to manipulation? The best interest of children and their testimony. *Children and Youth Services Review 51*:101–107. https://doi.org/10.1016/j.childyouth.2015.02.003

Comack E and Brickey S (2007) Constituting the violence of crimainlised women. *Canadian Journal of Criminology and Criminal Justice*, 49(1), 1–36.

Corston, J. (2007). *The Corston report: A review of women with particular vulnerabilities in the criminal justice system*. London: Home Office.

Corvo K, Dutton D and Chen W (2009) Do Duluth model interventions with perpetrators of domestic violence violate mental health professional ethics? *Ethics & Behavior 19*(4), 323–340. https://doi.org/10.1080/10508420903035323

Crown Prosecution Service (2021) Rape and Sexual Offences: Key Legislation, https://www.cps.gov.uk/legal-guidance/rape-and-sexual-offences-chapter-7-key-legislation-and-offences.

Curtis J (2019) Woman, 65, who killed her husband with a hammer after decades of abuse weeps in court as she has her 2011 murder conviction overturned in watershed moment for 'coercive control' law. *Daily Mail,* 1 March. Available at https://www.dailymail.co.uk/news/article-6756499/Wife-65-killed-husband-hammer-freed.html (accessed 1 March 2019).

Daly K (1994) *Gender, crime and punishment*. New Haven, CT: Yale University Press.

Dempsey B (2011) Gender neutral laws and heterocentric policies: 'Domestic abuse as gender-based abuse' and same-sex couples. *Edinburgh Law Review 15*(3): 381–390.

Domestic Abuse Act (2021) https://www.gov.uk/government/publications/domestic-abuse-bill-2020-factsheets/domestic-abuse-bill-2020-overarching-factsheet.

Douglas H, Tarrant, S and Tolmie J (2021) Social entrapment evidence: Understanding its role in self-defence cases involving intimate partner violence. *UNSW Law Journal, 44*(1), 326–356.

Dutton MA and Goodman LA (2005) Coercion in intimate partner violence: Toward a new conceptualization. *Sex Roles 52*(11): 743–756.

Edmunson, W. (1995) Is law coercive? *Legal Theory*, 1, 81–111.

Gardner RA (1992) *The parental alienation syndrome: A guide for mental health and legal professionals*. Cresskill, NJ: Creative Therapeutics.

Gelsthorpe L and Russel J (2018) Women and penal reform: Two steps forwards, three steps backwards? *The Political Quarterly 89*(2): 227–236.

Hanna C (2009) The paradox of progress: Translating Evan Stark's coercive control into legal doctrine for abused women. *Violence against Women 15*(2):1458–1476.

Heidensohn F (1996) *Women and crime* (2nd ed.). Basingstoke: Macmillan.

Himma KE (2020) *Coercion and the nature of the law*. Oxford: Oxford University Press.

Hulley S (2021) Defending 'co-offending' women: Recognising domestic abuse and coercive control in 'joint enterprise' cases involving women and their intimate partners. *The Howard Journal of Criminal Justice*. https://doi.org/ 10.111/hojo.12445

Koons-Witt B and Schram PJ (2003) The prevalence and nature of violent offending by females. *Journal of Criminal Justice 31*(4): 361–371.

Kuennen T.L (2007) Analyzing the impact of coercion on domestic violence victims: How much is too much. *Berkeley Journal of Gender, Law & Justice 22*(1), 1–30.

Lamond G (2000) The coerciveness of law. *Oxford Journal of Legal Studies 20*(1): 39–62.

Loveless J (2010) Domestic violence, coercion and duress. *Criminal Law Review* 233–256.

Madhok S, Phillips A and Wilson K (2013) *Gender, agency and coercion*. London: Palgrave/Macmillan.

Marital coercion (2014) *Anti-Social Bhevaiour, Crime and Policing Act*, legislation.gov.uk.

Meyer S (2012) Why women stay: A theoretical examination of rational choice and moral reasoning in the context of intimate partner violence. *Australian and New Zealand Journal of Criminology*, 45 (2), 179–193.

Midson B (2016) Coercive control and criminal responsibility: Victims who kill their abusers. *Criminal Law Reform 27*(4): 417–442.

Ministry of Justice (2019) *Female Offender Strategy*. London: HMSO.

Morrison F (2015) All over now? Ongoing relational consequences of domestic abuse thorough children's contact arrangements. *Child Abuse Review 24*(4): 274–294.

Mullins C and Wright R (2003) Gender social networks and residential burglary. *Criminology* 41(3): 813–840.

Pence E and Paymar M (1993) *Education groups for men who batter: The Duluth model*. New York, NY: Springer.

Pender RL (2012) ASGW best practice guidelines: an evaluation of the Duluth model. *The Journal for Specialists in Group Work 37*(3): 218–231.

Prison Reform Trust (2017) *'There's a reason we're in trouble': Domestic abuse as a driver to women's offending*. Prison Reform Trust Report.

Richie BE (1996) *Compelled to crime: The gender entrapment of battered black women*. New York, NY: Routledge.

Sheehy E.A., Stubbs J and Tolmie J. (2015) Securing fair outcomes for battered women charged with homicide: Analysing defence lawyering in R. v. Falls, *Melbourne University Law Review*, 38, 666–701.

Sheehy L (2018) Expert evidence on coercive control in support of self-defence: The trial of Teresa Craig. *Criminology & Criminal Justice 18*(1): 100–114.

Stark E (2007) *Coercive control: How men entrap women in personal life*. London: Oxford University Press.

Stover CS, Meadows AL and Kaufman J (2009) Interventions for intimate partner violence: Review and implications for evidence-based practice. *Professional Psychology: Research and Practice 40*(3): 223–233.

Sundari A and Gill A (2009) Coercion, consent and forced marriage debate in the UK. *Feminist Legal Studies 17*(2):165–184.

Tarrant S, Tolmie J and Giudce G (2019) Transforming legal understandings of intimate partner violence (ANROWS Research report, 03/2019). Sydney: ANROWS.

Tolmie J (2018) Coercive control: To criminalise or not to criminalise? *Criminology & Criminal Justice, 18*(1): 50–66.

Walker LE (1980) *The battered woman*. New York, NY: Harper & Row.

Walklate S, Fitz-Gibbon K and McCulloch J (2018) Is more law the answer? Seeking justice for victims of intimate partner violence through the reform of legal categories. *Criminology & Criminal Justice 18*(1), 115–131. https://doi.org/10.1177/1748895817728561

Welle D and Falkin G (2000) The everyday policing of women with romantic co-defendants: An ethnographic perspective. *Women and Criminal Justice 11*(2): 45–65.

3 Coercive control and victimization

Introduction

As discussed in Chapter 1, the presence of coercive control in intimate partner relationships and the gendered nature of this abuse has long been recognized (Schechter, 1982; Johnson, 1995; Stark, 2007; Pitman, 2017). The most influential understanding of this concept, particularly in the Anglo-speaking world, is Stark's (2007) work. Taking this influential work as a starting point, this chapter will consider the presence of coercive control as a strategy of victimization and its increasing influence in policy as one way of making sense of intimate partner abuse. In endeavouring to put coercive control in the context of abusive relationships, this chapter also considers two tricky but related questions: what constitutes a 'normal' relationship and when does coercion become controlling? In addition, coercive control, as articulated by Stark, is presented as gendered. This chapter will consider the efficacy of this view and will also explore the extent to which, as a concept, it captures the experiences of women in marginalized communities, especially those marked by structural inequalities (such as race, Indigeneity, immigration status, disability, and sexuality). First, we will provide a summary of the history of this way of thinking about intimate partner abuse.

The rise of coercive control in making sense of intimate partner abuse

Historically, domestic abuse was viewed as a 'private issue' that should be dealt with in the family home. The term *intimate partner abuse*, now perhaps more commonly referred to as domestic abuse though in some jurisdictions the term *family violence* is preferred, was not widely used in the United Kingdom. For example, in the 1960s, the term *wife battering*

DOI: 10.4324/9781003019114-3

was a more commonly used concept. Of course, it is now well recognized that this term, even when in use, limited the vision of intimate partner abuse to those who were married, excluding many other relationships. However, what has come to be referred as the second-wave feminist movement challenged this vision and drew attention to the endemic gendered nature of domestic and sexual violence (Dobash and Dobash, 1979). At that time, of course, domestic abuse was not seen to be a serious issue neither by the criminal justice system nor social services more generally. This quote from the International Association of Police Chiefs Training Manual from the 1960s exemplifies this:

> For the most part these disputes are personal matters requiring no direct police action. ... In dealing with family disputes the power of arrest should be exercised as a last resort. The officer should never create a police problem when there is only a family problem existing.
>
> (cited in Dobash and Dobash, 1979:10)

In England and Wales and elsewhere, things have changed since this time. Her Majesty's Inspectorate of Constabulary's, 'Increasingly Everyone's Business' report (HMIC, 2015) stated that policing domestic abuse is 'a huge and important responsibility. It is critical that the police fulfil it successfully for the victims that they serve'. From the 2000s onwards, England and Wales, as elsewhere, has seen a significant expansion in resource and provision provided for domestic-related crimes, including specialist domestic abuse courts, police domestic abuse risk assessment tools, the introduction of the Domestic Violence Disclosure Scheme (Clare's Law)[1], Domestic Violence Protection Notices/Orders (DVPN/Os)[2], and the expansion of the civil law (including non-molestation orders) and criminal law (including the criminalization of coercive and controlling behaviours). Other jurisdictions (notably the United States, Canada, Australia, and New Zealand among others) have similarly devoted a good deal of energy and resources to the problem of domestic abuse since the 1960s.

A fundamental shift in understanding about the nature, extent, and impact of domestic abuse has also taken place during this time period. This is the recognition that abuse does not have to be physical to cause significant harm to victims. Historically, domestic abuse was equated with physical violence, and as has already been intimated, terms such as *wife battering* were commonly used to describe such abuse. Settling on an agreed term for such abuse, however, is neither simple nor straightforward. During the 1980s, for example, the term domestic violence became increasingly used as a way of capturing the violent nature of some relationships as well as their private character. However, that term itself failed to satisfy all the voices concerned with this issue, since in its operationalization it still tended to exclude those not married and/or living together. The focus on physical violence in defining the acts under consideration and thereby informing practice has been particularly problematic. Indeed, definitions and the question of who does what to whom are pertinent to the discussion in relation to coercive control that follows. At this juncture, suffice it to say that for some time feminist critics have argued that legal conceptualizations of domestic abuse have hinged on single acts of physical violence. This focus obscures the nuances and complexity of such abuse and reduced the ability of victim/survivors to derive adequate protection for either themselves or their children resonant with their experiences.

The impacts of psychological, coercive, emotional, and controlling abusive behaviours were not understood until more recently, with Schechter (1982) arguably being the first to introduce the concept of coercive control. Such forms of abuse lead to feelings of entrapment, erosion of confidence, and self-esteem and limit a victim/survivor's space for action (Ptacek, 1999; Sharp-Jeffs et al., 2018). Coercive control and its impact have been discussed in Chapter 1; however, it is worth spending some time here reflecting on how understandings of the concept of coercive control have developed and changed in recent years.

For example, Johnson (2017) reflects on the ways in which his theory of intimate partner abuse has developed over time. His original work (1995) featured two types of intimate partner abuse: 'patriarchal terrorism' and 'ordinary couple violence'. Although the terminology has changed since, these concepts remain the same in his most recent iterations. 'Ordinary couple violence' captured the mutual violence perpetrated in intimate relationships by both parties. This was later changed to 'situational couple violence', as Johnson felt that the term *ordinary* minimized the seriousness of such abuse (Johnson, 2008). 'Patriarchal terrorism' described gendered, one-sided forms of abuse, deployed almost exclusively by men against women. This was later changed to 'coercive and controlling violence', greatly influenced by Stark's (2007) work. This concept captures the ways in which victims of such abuse, predominantly women, experience a form of intimate terrorism that is rooted in gendered and patriarchal motivations. According to Johnson (2017), this type of abuse is about both the use and threat of violence, in combination with other controlling tactics, to terrorize one's partner. Despite Johnson's body of work being among the first to develop a typology of intimate partner abuse, which centralized coercive and controlling behaviour in this way, his work has not gained the same international influence in policy and practice as Stark's (2007) work has done.

Stark's (2007) conceptualization of coercive control has had the most influence globally in understanding coercive control as a gendered course of conduct: repeated physical violence interspersed with control, intimidation, threats, and isolation. He suggests that coercive control is a liberty crime, in which a woman's freedom is limited both literally and symbolically through restricting her thoughts and behaviour. Stark (2007) likens women trapped in coercive and controlling relationships to a hostage situation, emphasizing the power imbalance, minimal capacity for autonomy, and difficulty in leaving the relationship. Stark's (2007) concept recognizes the harms caused by physical violence and assault but stresses it is the cumulative impact of the range of coercive and controlling techniques that perpetrators use, whether physical violence or not, which has a long-term effect on victims, likening the harms caused to that of post-traumatic stress disorder. He emphasizes the harms associated with psychological, emotional, coercive, and economic abuse in particular.

Stark's (2007) conceptualization has influenced international policy, including in England and Wales, Scotland, Australia, Denmark, Ireland and the USA, with some of these jurisdictions criminalizing coercive and controlling behaviour using his vision. (The issues associated with the criminalization of coercive control and implementation of such offences are discussed further in Chapter 4.) There are various reasons why Stark's (2007) work specifically has grasped the public policy agenda since it was first published. Firstly, Stark's work has a clinical basis. The approach within it is therapeutic in orientation and lends itself well to practice interventions. Second, defining coercive control as a liberty crime positions it firmly within the criminal justice domain, particularly when this is set in the context of the rising global focus on human rights. Third, his concept entered the international policy scene when global concern about violence against women was also on the rise and has benefitted from the global processes and influences of the United States in what Goodmark (2015) has termed *exporting without a license.* Put simply, the exporting of US policies and practices to address violence against women globally. This uncritical exportation of US law and policy is problematic. US policy on domestic abuse itself has not been particularly effective in decreasing such violence, and the exportation of Stark's concept to other jurisdictions ignores differences in social and cultural contexts, as well as broader social problems that contribute to domestic abuse. These issues will be discussed further in later chapters.

Finally, the translation of coercive control into policy and law offers a simple solution to a complex problem for policy makers. Adding more law allows policy makers and governing representatives to appear to be doing 'something' about violence against women, while avoiding having to spend significant time, energy, and money on other much needed investments (discussed further in Chapters 4 and 5).

Recognizing these processes as the context in which coercive control has risen on the policy agenda is important, since at the same time these processes render invisible at least two assumptions embedded in this concept. First, the assumption that the women who are in such relationships understand and recognize this behaviour as abusive and that a line can be easily drawn between 'normal' persuasive behaviour in relationships and coercively controlling behaviour. Second, that experiences of coercion are monolithic, rather than being differently shaped by the impact of structural inequalities and marginalization. These two issues are explored in what follows.

When does control become coercive?

The value of coercive control as a clinical concept is significant, providing victim-survivors with a meaningful way of understanding their experiences of ongoing strategies of intimidation, isolation, and control extending to all areas of their life depriving them of their liberty. However, for coercive control to be effectively translated into law and policy, there needs to be clear distinctions between when behaviours become controlling *and* coercive. Arguably, all relationships involve persuasion and/or influence (Dutton and Goodman, 2005). For example, one person in a relationship may have greater control over the finances, but this could be because they are better at managing money than their partner. Or one person may try to regulate the alcohol intake of the other, because when their partner is intoxicated it disrupts the children and family routine. A key feature of a relationship being *coercive* and controlling is the presence of fear, that is, one person (usually a woman) restricts, changes, or limits their behaviour in response to a partner's demands because they are afraid of them. For instance, in the example mentioned above, if the person was afraid to access their finances freely, then this arguably constitutes coercive control. A useful way of thinking about whether the behaviour is coercive or not is the pressure that has been exerted on us to behave in a particular way and whether this is more than the pressures we all face in relationships (Kuennen, 2007). In the former example, having limited or no access to their own finances can certainly be viewed as constituting more pressure than what many people face depending on individual circumstances. Pointedly, the nature of the circumstances matters.

Of significance to this discussion is who decides when and what behaviours are coercive and controlling? Victim-survivors should be the key informant, and decades of feminist scholarship has highlighted the importance of listening to women's voices in, for example, recognizing women's ability to assess their own levels of risk in the context of domestic abuse (Barlow and Walklate, 2021; Barlow et al., 2020). However, the identification of behaviours as coercive in intimate relationships becomes more complex when it is considered whether women recognize their experiences as such. Victims-survivors of coercive control often occupy a false world created by the perpetrator, unable to freely make their own choices or live their lives autonomously. Gaslighting, isolation, and deprivation often prevent women understanding experiences within their relationship as abusive (Bettinson and Bishop, 2015). Perpetrators will often use specific techniques that are unique to the victim and relationship to coercively control the victim, making it difficult for third parties to identify and understand what is going on. This is particularly the case when elements of a relationship are viewed in isolation rather than as a wider pattern of abuse. Such behaviour may seem trivial to someone outside the relationship, and it is often difficult for victims to articulate the magnitude and impact of what is happening to them. Furthermore, many victim-survivors may not recognize their partner as abusive at all if there is no physical violence present, as physical violence is often more readily associated with domestic abuse in comparison with control and psychological abuse (Gill, 2004). Herein lie some of the difficulties in translating this concept into law, where a judge must determine and draw the lines between 'normal' persuasion in relationships and coercive control when such distinctions are often complex for victim-survivors themselves to identify. The complexities associated with criminalizing coercive control are discussed further in Chapter 4.

It is additionally problematic for other people, particularly state representatives, to tell women what they are experiencing is coercive control, especially when their intervention is uninvited. The issues with state interference in women's lives and women's resistance to this are well documented. State actors, perhaps unintentionally, often fail to appreciate the social and cultural contexts of many women's real lives with law and policy emanating from a monolithic view of lived experience. For example, in Indigenous societies, exposure of abuse to anyone outside the family and community is viewed with great distain, with maintaining the support of one's family viewed as being more important

(Kuennen, 2007). For some women, although coercive control is a significant source of harm in their lives, it is not the only source of harm. State intervention can potentially be seen as more harmful for themselves, their family, and their community.

The potential for blurred distinctions between persuasion and coercion in relationships, with victim-survivors not always recognizing their experiences as abuse is, at least in part, exacerbated by a lack of a clear, unified definition of coercion in understandings of coercive control. Schechter's (1982) definition included threats, emotional insults, and economic deprivation. Stark (2007) pointed to strategies of intimidation, isolation, and control as comprising coercive control. Although both definitions have clear similarities, and both offer useful exemplar behaviours, they do not include a clear definition of coercion itself. Given the efforts to translate this concept into law and policy, this lack of clarity presents some issues (this has also been discussed in relation to offending in Chapter 2). Nevertheless, Dutton and Goodman (2005) have attempted to define coercion within the context of intimate partner abuse specifically. They suggest that it is a dynamic process in which an abuser makes a demand and threatens a negative consequence for non-compliance with the demand. As highlighted by Kuennen (2007), this definition focuses on the process of coercion itself, rather than drawing attention to exemplar behaviours, such as isolation and intimidation. This distinction is important, as it allows consideration of the role of the victim-survivor and the extent to which she is free to make a choice herself in such contexts. There is also a clear distinction between coercion and force in Dutton and Goodman's (2005) definition, as it is the threat of negative consequences that is emphasized rather than physical force. These are important nuances when translating such concepts into law. As discussed in Chapter 2, coercion is not in reality a dichotomous experience, even though it is articulated this way in law (you are either coerced or not). Rather it exists on a continuum (Barlow, 2016). For example, for some women, the threat of murder or threat of taking away her children may be viewed as more coercive than the threat of being humiliated in front of family and friends. However, both are examples of coercion specifically rather than force, as there is no physical element in either, rather the threat of such.

A further key issue when conceptualizing coercive control is context. As highlighted by Kuennen (2007: 13), 'in trying to understand the dynamics of coercive control, context is everything'. When an abuser coerces a victim, she has a choice to comply, resist, or a mixture of both. However, this is not a 'free choice', and the context in which this decision is made is fundamental (Dutton and Goodman, 2005). For example, a woman who is employed and has good access to resources may have a greater ability to resist coercion (particularly if she feels able and ready to leave the relationship) as opposed to a migrant woman who has no legal status to remain in the current country of residence. This is not to minimize any experiences of coercion, but it is rather to highlight the importance of context in understanding the process of coercion and the woman's ability to exercise any level of agency within this process. Acknowledging women's capacity for choice in such contexts, and the structural constraints that may limit such choices, is important. It is important to acknowledge a victim's capacity to survive, hence the term *survivor*. Women can and do leave violent relationships, and to understand the role of coercion within this context, we need to recognize women's capacity for autonomy, irrespective of the impossible positions they may find themselves in.

Kuennen (2007) discussed such issues in relation to survivor decisions as to whether they support the prosecution of their abuser. If legal advocates and judges believe that a decision to drop a case is because the woman has been coerced by an abuser, it can add to the reluctance on the part of criminal justice professionals to give credence to her decision. Here she is highlighting a fundamental tension between legal understandings of choice and those understandings based on experience. In so doing, Kuennen's (2007) observations sensitize us to the ongoing failure to view intimate partner abuse, and its impact, through the eyes of its victim-survivors and what the policy implications might be for trying to take their vision into account. For example, understanding that choice (usually to withdraw a complaint) is not necessarily a 'free' choice might assist police officers in understanding how and why victim attrition in cases such as these occurs. Further, this kind of shift in focus would place courts in a better position to appreciate the 'voluntariness' of a victim's decision. The ways in which external pressures influence women's choices, such as concerns over children being taken away, unwanted interference of the state and criminal justice system, and structural inequalities with which many women routinely live, are all part of understanding the nature of coercive control in their lives.

To summarize, the need for clear definitions of coercive control and the importance of understanding the context in which coercive control occurs are both important factors to consider when understanding coercive control as a strategy of victimization. However, Stark's (2007) conceptualization and its subsequent influence in law and criminal justice policy in jurisdictions across the globe does not necessarily capture the more complex dynamics of coercive control experienced by women already marginalized by the criminal justice process. These issues are discussed in the next section of the chapter.

Structural inequalities, marginalized women, and coercive control

Sokoloff and Dupont (2005) critique universal approaches to understanding women's experiences, suggesting that understandings of domestic abuse focusing predominantly on white women's experiences, which arguably much of the work discussed in this chapter so far does, consequently exclude all experiences that fall outside these structural characteristics. Kanuha (1996: 40) argues that the implication that domestic abuse affects 'every person, across race, class, nationally and religious lines' equally is 'not only a token attempt at inclusion of diverse perspectives, but also evidence of sloppy research and theory building'. Intersectional thinking argues that traditional feminist understandings of violence against women downplay the influence of structural dimensions and the ways in which these intersect with gender. The fact that domestic abuse is highly gendered does not mean that all women are affected in the same way, but rather structural variables, such as race, culture, Indigenous status, socio-economic circumstances, insecure immigration status, and disability reinforce the oppression they experience as a function of intimate partner abuse (Goodmark, 2018; Sokoloff and Dupont, 2005; Canning, 2020). Stark's (2007) theorization of coercive control does not fully engage with these nuances. Gender is importantly central in his conceptualization, but the ways in which gender intersects with other structural constraints to produce multiple inequalities and barriers for women experiencing coercive control is not fully explored. Moreover, as we shall see, it also fails to consider men.

To date, the introduction of the coercive and controlling behaviour offence in England and Wales and other jurisdictions does not take into account the structural problems associated with intimate partner abuse. The increased emphasis on the criminalization of coercive control sends out a strong societal message that such behaviour will not be tolerated and provides an avenue of support for those victim-survivors who wish to engage with the criminal justice system (discussed further in Chapter 4). However, the implications of the criminalization process for marginalized groups and the different ways in which such women may experience coercion in relationships require further consideration. These are discussed in what follows.

Black and minority ethnic and Indigenous women

Marginalized people are the most harmed by an overreliance on criminal justice approaches, particularly black and minority ethnic people and Indigenous people (Blagg, 2008). Women of colour and Indigenous women are less likely to voluntarily enter the criminal justice system as a result of fears of racism and discrimination for both themselves and their partner. These concerns added layers to the hostility they may experience from criminal justice professionals and raise questions concerning their exposure to greater risk of state violence and control (Sokoloff and Dupont, 2005; Goodmark, 2018; Blagg, 2008). Coker (2001) suggests that state intervention and criminalization can cause more intrusion and harm for poor black and minority ethnic women, with increasing risks of arrest for the victim themselves and unwanted removal of children by the state. It is evident that women expend considerable energy and time battling 'the system' and the state, and this highlights the ways in which women's space for action can be constrained by structural barriers (Sharp-Jeffs et al., 2018). An emphasis on criminal justice approaches is therefore likely to exclude such women's experiences and lead to further marginalization. Such complexities are particularly exacerbated for migrant women and those seeking asylum (Bosworth and Turnbull, 2015).

Migrant women

There are many and varied cultural and structural barriers that migrant women experience when seeking support for domestic abuse. Some examples include language barriers, geographic isolation from friends and family members, lack of access to public funds, economic dependency on their partner or the state, unstable legal and immigration status, lack of knowledge of the support available, and using their home country as a frame of reference for the justice system (Graca, 2021). It is therefore not surprising that migrant and asylum-seeking women tend to avoid interacting with the criminal justice system when experiencing abuse in their intimate relationship. Graca (2018) explores the ways in which migrant women deal with experiences of abuse in the absence of criminal justice interventions highlighting that they tend to prefer adopting inconspicuous and informal approaches to protect themselves from abuse, such as hiding the abuse, seeking support from friends and family where possible, or taking steps to adapt their behaviour to avoid abuse. Although such behaviours may seem passive, Graca (2018) argued that these were viewed by the women themselves as forms of resistance, as their greatest fear was bringing state intervention into their private lives. This point is important, particularly when referring to earlier discussions regarding what constitutes 'normal' or accepted levels of control in relationships, and how this may vary by cultural and social circumstance. However, this also raises important points regarding women's capacity for, albeit limited, agency even when experiencing coercive control. Thus, for migrant women, who have to navigate their varied and complex social and cultural conditions, state interference is feared to such an extent that they develop their own forms of resistance within the context of their relationship to avoid interaction with the criminal justice system (Graca, 2021).

Canning (2020) goes further and discusses the ways in which the punitive landscape of Britain's asylum system facilitates further violence against women seeking asylum, rather than providing protection. These observations draw attention to the coercive nature of the state itself. She develops the concept of 'corrosive control' to highlight the ways in which the structures of coercive control in intimate relationships are replicated by the state and its amorphous relations with corporations. Maher and Segrave (2018) similarly identified that for migrant women living in Victoria, Australia, any 'vulnerabilities' such women experienced were predominantly created by service and legislative regimes. They caution that, rather than assuming such vulnerabilities are inherent for migrant women, there needs to be better recognition of the women's own assessments of risk and their searches for safety.

Women with disabilities

Women with disabilities are also negatively impacted by an emphasis on criminalisation. For these women in experiencing domestic abuse, they are likely to experience additional barriers and abusive techniques. For example, they are often more reliant on their abuser (commonly, their partner) for personal assistance with daily, and perhaps intimate, care tasks, often increasing their vulnerability and lack of safety (Nosek et al., 2001). Perpetrators frequently abuse their partners in ways that increase the powerfulness of their own position, making use of, and exploiting, the woman's impairment or condition. For example, a qualitative UK study by Magowan (2004) explored how disabled women's increased vulnerability interacted with the mechanisms of abusive relationships to give rise to new types of violence and to more complex barriers to escape. Various barriers to seeking criminal justice support have been identified for such women, including not having other options (particularly if the perpetrator is their main carer), not trusting agencies to respond effectively, and fear of losing their independence or children and personal pride (Radford et al., 2006; Thiara et al., 2011). Nixon (2009) has referred to the cumulative effect of these processes as 'compound oppressions', which focus attention on the intersection of disadvantage on the grounds of both disability and other factors, such as gender.

Sexualities

Compounded impacts of coercive control have also been noted by Donovan and Hester (2014) in relation to same-sex relationships. They argue that an unintended consequence of the success of feminist scholarship and activism around violence against women has been the construction of a particular public story of intimate partner abuse. This constructs such abuse as a problem of heterosexual men for heterosexual women, a problem primarily of physical violence, and a problem of a particular presentation of gender: a big 'strong' man being physically violent towards a small 'weak' woman. While this public story reflects some of the empirical evidence about who is most often victimized by intimate partner abuse, it nevertheless makes it very difficult for those whose experiences do not fit with it to either tell their story or be heard. Namely, it excludes not only those who are LGB (lesbian, gay, bisexual) and/or T+ (transgender) but also heterosexual men, and any victim, regardless of sexuality or gender identity, whose experience is not primarily of physical violence (Donovan and Barnes, 2019).

There is less work exploring the impact of coercive control in same-sex relationships when compared with heterosexual partnerships. However, Frankland and Brown (2014) found that around one-quarter of their survey sample of 184 same-sex couples used coercive and controlling behaviours, and this was particularly present in male same-sex relationships. They noted high levels of sexual coercion and physical violence in particular. Raghavan et al. (2019) surveyed 126 men in same-sex relationships about their experiences of coercive control and also reported high levels of physical violence, interwoven with non-physical abusive techniques such as punishment and intimation. They highlighted that the men in the study were less likely to experience deprivation and micro-regulation when compared with the literature exploring heterosexual relationships. Moreover, both studies highlighted the reluctance of same-sex male and female victims to engage with the criminal justice system.

Collectively, this body of work highlights that although gender is central to understanding the experience and prevalence of intimate partner abuse and specifically coercive control, additional structural constraints also need to be considered to understand the ways in which multiple inequalities can impact victim-survivor experiences of coercive control and the likelihood of help-seeking. Furthermore, the previously discussed work concerning male same-sex victims of coercive control highlights the need to explore men's experiences of victimization in greater depth.

Men, victimization, and coercive control

Much of the work on coercive control has identified that such experiences are gendered. Put simply, this takes as given the view that it is male perpetrators who victimize females. Indeed, empirical evidence on abuse, generally, and coercive control, specifically, points to evidence that these behaviours are for the most part perpetrated by men against women. However, much of this work emanates from different conceptual starting points, using differently constituted data samples, and with different visions of intervention in mind (see inter alia Robertson and Murachver, 2011). General observations such as these notwithstanding, men are victims of abuse and coercive control. Recognizing this does not negate the clear gendered dimensions of coercive control, but rather strengthens understandings of the impacts and harms of such abuses and how this is differently experienced by men and women. However, the question remains as to what men's experiences of such victimization look like, and what the impact of them might be. One place in which to start is within understandings of men and their relationship with masculinity.

Some time ago, Messerschmidt (1993: 150) observed:

> Wife beating/rape is a specific practice designed with an eye to one's accountability as a 'real man' and, therefore, serves as a suitable resource for simultaneously accomplishing gender and affirming patriarchal masculinity.

Taking this as a starting point facilitates an appreciation of the extent to which being victimized can and does challenge a man's sense of himself as a man. Situating men's experiences within understandings of masculinity can make sense of not only how they understand those experiences but also how, when they ask for help, if they do, they are responded to.

Early work on men's experiences of victimization in general clearly points to the reluctance of men to give expression to such experiences (see inter alia Stanko and Hobdell, 1993). At the same time, when they do give voices to such experiences, these experiences are unlikely to provoke expressions of fear and vulnerability. As Machado et al. (2016) point out, the men in their sample simply did not recognize their experiences as victimization nor did they seek help. In addition, Javaid (2018: 200) observed in connection with his empirical work on male victims of rape,

> Men are not expected to be victims, vulnerable, hurt, damaged, emotional and sensitive; by enacting these traits, however, they are not achieving hegemonic masculinity and are not seen as 'real' men.

Though as Halsey (2018: 443) points out, even among those hardened and committed to becoming feared, 'there are small fissures in everyone's subjectivity'. Such fissures might be exposed by asking men different questions (as Stanko, 1990, found in her work on personal safety). Walker et al. (2020) in their study explored behaviours that men considered to be 'boundary crossing' (for example, impeding their right to safety, privacy, self-esteem). In their sample, 55.4% of men talked of a pattern of abusive behaviours, which for them constituted boundary crossing. These behaviours included physical, sexual, and controlling abuses, which for some also included undermining their relationship with their children. Over 90% of these men told a friend or a family member about this abuse to be met with very mixed responses. Other work has gone on to document the impact of this kind of abuse on men. Expressed by Bates (2020) as 'walking on eggshells', by Westmarland et al. (2021) as 'living a life by permission', with Bates and Carthy (2020) drawing particular attention to the impact that such abuse has on older men – 'she had me believing I had Alzheimer's'. In sum, Graham-Kevan et al. (2021) suggest that the impact of these kinds of behaviours (all of which fit in the rubric of coercive control) resulted in eight out of ten men in their sample displaying symptoms not unlike post-traumatic distress.

In the context of men's experience of violence(s) and control in their interpersonal relationships, the fissures Halsey (2018) refers to above frequently, though not always, coalesce around children and access to children when separating or already separated from their partner. It is perhaps no great coincidence that men's voices have become increasingly present in relation to their experience of such separation issues as the men's movement has also grown (Durfee, 2011). Nevertheless, the using of children as a weapon of control, by both men and women, and the different ways in which this can manifest itself, needs to be recognized (Harman et al., 2020).

To summarize, men remain unlikely to frame their interpersonal experiences in terms of domestic and/or family violence. Neither are they likely to express fear in the face of their experiences. Indeed such fears are likely more associated with them not being seen as masculine if they do disclose alongside the real fear that they would be met with disbelief by those who they disclose to, particularly criminal justice professionals (Migliaccio, 2001). Nevertheless, this does not mean that they lie outside the experience of coercive control, but it does mean that such experiences are perhaps in need of closer scrutiny. For example, in a recent study by Policastro and Finn (2021), they reported that the 'odds of men being subjected to surveillance by their intimate partners were significantly higher that females'. Of course, making sense of findings such as these, and the causal mechanisms that underpin them, is open to ongoing debate and investigation.

Conclusion

Coercive control is incredibly harmful behaviour that has significant and dangerous impacts on women and children. Stark's (2007) conceptualization provides a powerful clinical concept, allowing women to make sense of their experiences of violence and abuse in their intimate relationships. However, as outlined in this chapter, the concept is not without its limitations and the complexities it overlooks, particularly in terms of whose experiences it captures. These include the lack of a clear distinction between 'normal' pressure in an intimate relationship and coercive control, the importance of developing a clearer definition of the process of coercion itself, the need to consider the nuance of context and the capacity for women to be able to make choices, albeit limited, within the context of coercion, among being able to catalogue the diverse experiences associated with coercive control. The policy response of criminalization provoked as a result of the influence of Stark's work is also not without its problems. The process of criminalization implies a monolithic experience of coercive control, when the reality is much more complex and which can often be difficult for the victim/survivors themselves to articulate. Greater involvement of the state in women's lives as a result of the processes of criminalization can have considerable negative consequences for those whose lives are marred by structural inequalities. Chapter 4 will consider some of the implications of some of these nuances and the policy response of criminalization more broadly in greater depth.

Notes

1 The first Domestic Violence Disclosure Scheme (DVDS) (Clare's Law) was rolled out across England and Wales in March 2014. Such schemes comprise two elements: a right to ask (a request made by any member of the public for information about whether a person has a history of violence) and a right to know (police proactively requesting disclosure of information to protect a 'high risk' victim from harm from their partner).
2 A DVPO is a civil order that enables police and magistrates' courts to put protective measures in place in the immediate aftermath of domestic abuse where there is insufficient evidence to charge a perpetrator. A DVPN is an emergency non-molestation eviction notice that can be issued by police when attending a domestic abuse case. Within 48 hours of a DVPN being served on a perpetrator, an application by police to the magistrates' court must be heard.

References

Barlow C (2016) *Coercion and women co-offenders: A gendered pathway into crime.* Bristol: Policy Press.

Barlow C, Johnson J, Walklate S and Humphreys L (2020) Putting coercive control into practice: Problems and possibilities. *The British Journal of Criminology 60*(1): 160–179.

Barlow C and Walklate S (2021) Gender, risk assessment and coercive control: Contradictions in terms? *The British Journal of Criminology 61*(4): 887–904. https://doi.org/10.1093/bjc/azaa104

Bates EA (2020) 'Walking on egg shells': A qualitative examination of men's experiences of intimate partner violence. *Psychology of Men & Masculinities 21*(1), 13–24.

Bates EA and Carthy NL (2020) 'She convinced me I had Alzheimer's': Experiences of intimate partner violence in older men. *Psychology of Men & Masculinities 21*(4), 675–685.

Bettinson V and Bishop C (2015) Is the creation of a discrete offence of coercive control necessary to combat domestic violence? *Northern Ireland Legal Quarterly 66*(2): 179–197.

Blagg H (2008) *Crime, Aboriginality and the decolonisation of justice.* Leichardt: Hawkins Press.

Bosworth M and Turnbull S (2015) Immigration detention and the expansion of penal power in the United Kingdom. In Reiter K and Koenig A (Eds.), *Extraordinary punishment: An empirical look at administrative black holes in the United States and Canada* (pp. 50–67). London: Palgrave.

Canning V (2020) Corrosive control: State-corporate and gendered harm in bordered Britain. *Critical Criminology 28*: 259–275.

Coker D (2001) Crime control and feminist law reform in domestic violence law: A critical review. *Buffalo Criminal Law Review 4*(2), 801–860.

Dobash RE and Dobash RP (1979) *Violence against wives: A case against the patriarchy*. New York, NY: Free Press.

Donovan C and Hester M (2014) *Domestic violence and sexuality: What's love got to do with it?* Bristol: Policy Press.

Donovan C and Barnes R (2019) Retangling the concept of coercive control: A view from the margins and a response to Walby and Towers (2018). *Criminology and Criminal Justice 21*(2), 242–257.

Durfee A (2011) 'I'm not a victim, she's an abuser': masculinity, victimization, and protection orders. *Gender & Society 25*(3): 316–334. http://dx.doi.org/10.1177/0891243211404889

Dutton MA and Goodman LA (2005) Coercion in intimate partner violence: Toward a new conceptualization. *Sex Roles 52*(11), 743–756.

Frankland A and Brown J (2014) Coercive control in same-sex intimate partner violence. *Journal of Family Violence 29*(1): 15–22.

Gill A (2004) South Asian women's experiences of domestic violence. *The Howard Journal of Criminal Justice 43*(5), 465–483.

Goodmark L (2015) Exporting without license: The American attempt to end intimate partner abuse worldwide. In Goel R and Goodmark L (Eds.), *Comparative perspectives on gender violence: Lessons from efforts worldwide* (pp. 3–14). Oxford: Oxford University Press.

Goodmark L (2018) *Decriminalizing domestic violence: A balanced policy approach to intimate partner violence*. Oakland, CA: University of California Press.

Graca S (2018) Domestic violence policy and legislation in the UK: A discussion of immigrant women's vulnerabilities. *European Journal of Current Legal Issues 22*(1).

Graca S (2021) Resistance and the paradox of legal entitlement: A theoretical analysis of migrant women's responses to domestic abuse in the host country. *The Journal of Legal Pluralism and Unofficial Law 53*(2): 290–314. https://10.1080/07329113.2021.1925458

Graham-Kevan N, Powney D and Mankind (2021) *Male victims of coercive control: Experiences and impact*. UCLAN: Criminal Justice Partnership.

Halsey M (2018) Becoming feared: fashioning and projecting the violence self. In Lee M and Mythen G (Eds.), *Routledge international handbook on the fear of crime* (pp. 429–446). London: Routledge.

Harman JJ, Lorandos D, Biringen Z *et al.* (2020). Gender differences in the use of parental alienating behaviors. *Journal of Family Violence 35*: 459–469. https://doi.org/10.1007/s10896-019-00097-5

Her Majesty's Inspectorate Constabulary (2015) *Increasingly everybody's business*. London: HMIC.

Javaid A (2018) Male rape, masculinities and sexualities. *International Journal of Law, Crime and Justice 52*: 199–210.

Johnson MP (1995) Patriarchal terrorism and common couple violence: Two forms of violence against women. *Journal of Marriage and the Family 57*: 283–294.

Johnson MP (2008) *A typology of domestic violence: Intimate terrorism, violent resistance, and situational couple violence.* Boston, MA: Northeastern University Press.

Johnson MP (2017) A personal social history of a typology of intimate partner violence. *Journal of Family Theory and Review 9*(2):150–164. https://doi.org/10.1111/jftr.12187

Kanuha V (1996) Domestic violence, racism and the battered women's movement in the United States. In Edleson JL and Eisxikovits ZC (Eds.), *Future interventions with battered women and their families* (pp. 34–50). Sage.

Kuennen TL (2007) Analyzing the impact of coercion on domestic violence victims: How much is too much. *Berkeley Journal of Gender, Law & Justice 22*(1).

Machado A, Hines D and Matos M (2016) Help-seeking and needs of male victims of intimate partner violence in Portugal. *Psychology of Men and Masculinity 17*(3), 255–264.

Magowan P (2004) *The impact of disability on women's experiences of domestic abuse: An empirical study into disabled women's experiences of and responses to domestic abuse.* ESRC PhD thesis.

Maher J and Segrave M (2018) Family violence risk, migration status and 'vulnerability': hearing the voices of immigrant women. *Journal of Gender-Based Violence 2*(3): 503–518.

Messerschmidt JW (1993) *Masculinities and crime.* Lanham, MD: Rowman & Littlefield.

Migliaccio TA (2001) Marginalizing the battered male. *The Journal of Men's Studies, 9*(2): 205–226. http://doi.org/10.3149/jms.0902.205

Nixon J (2009) Domestic violence and women with disabilities: Locating the issue on the periphery of social movements. *Disability and Society 24*(1), 77–89.

Nosek MA, Howland C and Chanpong GF (2001) National study of women with physical disabilities: Final report. *Sexuality and Disability 19*, 5–40.

Pitman T (2017) Living with coercive control: Trapped within a complex web of double standards, double binds and boundary violations. *British Journal of Social Work 47*(1): 143–161.

Policastro C and Finn MA (2021) Coercive control in intimate relationships: Differences across age and sex. *Journal of Interpersonal Violence 36*(3–4): 1520–1543.

Ptacek J (1999) *Battered women in the courtroom: The power of judicial responses.* Boston, MA: North Eastern University Press.

Radford L, Harne L and Trotter J (2006) Disabled women and domestic violence as violent crime in practice. *Journal of the British Association of Social Workers 18*(4): 56–72.

Raghavan C, Beck CJ, Menke JM and Loveland J (2019) Coercive controlling behaviours in intimate partner violence in male same-sex relationships: A mixed methods study. *Journal of Gay and Lesbian Social Services 31*(3): 370–395.

Robertson K and Murachver T (2011) Women and men's use of coercive control in intimate partner violence. *Violence and Victims 26*(3): 208–217.

Schechter S (1982) *Women and male violence: The visions and struggles of the Battered Women's Movement.* South End Press: Cambridge

Sharp-Jeffs N, Kelly L and Klein R (2018) Long journeys toward freedom: The relationship between coercive control and space for action: Measurement and emerging evidence. *Violence against Women 24*(2): 163–185.

Sokoloff NJ and Dupont I (2005) Domestic violence at the intersections of race, class and gender: Challenges and contributions to understanding violence against marginalised women in diverse communities. *Violence against Women 11*(1): 38–64.

Stanko B (1990) *Everyday violence.* London: Pandora.

Stanko E and Hobdell K (1993) Assault on men: masculinity and male victimization. *The British Journal of Criminology 33*(3), 400–415.

Stark E (2007) *Coercive control: How men entrap women in everyday life.* Oxford: Oxford University Press.

Thiara RK, Hague G and Mullender A (2011) Losing out on both counts: Disabled women and domestic violence. *Disabled & Society 26*(6): 757–771.

Walker, A., Lyall, K., Silva, D., Craigie, G., Mayshak, R., Costa, B., Hyder, S., and Bentley, A. (2020). Male victims of female-perpetrated intimate partner violence, help-seeking, and reporting behaviors: A qualitative study. *Psychology of Men & Masculinities 21*(2), 213–223.

Westmarland N, Burrell SR, Dhir A, Hall KE, Hasan E and Henderson K (2021) 'Living a life by permission': The experiences of male victims of domestic abuse during covid-19. Project Report. Durham University.

4 Criminalizing coercive control

Introduction

Since Stark (2007) defined coercive control as a 'liberty crime', much of the contemporary debate surrounding coercive control has been less concerned with whether it is a feature of domestic abuse or not (the previous chapters have indicated that it is), but more concerned with the extent to which there is a role for the (criminal) law in responding to this kind of abuse. Before proceeding to discuss the various ways in which different jurisdictions have endeavoured to criminalize coercive control, it is worth noting that the notion of a 'liberty crime' itself emanates from a very particular socio-legal context with its own traditions in respect of the relationship between citizenship, rights and the role of the local and federal state in both protecting and delivering these. Placing the notion of a liberty crime in its context immediately raises a question concerning the transferability of this vision of an appropriate response to coercive control from one criminal justice jurisdiction to another. Indeed, Sheley (2020) has pointed out that due process problems would be generated even in the United States in assuming the transferability of coercive control as a specific offence from one state to another. She concludes that the

> legal reformers who seek to use our increased understanding of the sociological reality of gender-based harm may be better served not to create specialized offenses to address it.
>
> (ibid.: 63)

Of course, it is the case that over the last 50 years or so views among academics, practitioners, and campaigners on the efficacy of the law as a response to domestic abuse more generally do differ. Some see the progressive potential in the criminal law (e.g., Lewis et al., 2001), with others

DOI: 10.4324/9781003019114-4

pointing to its unintended consequences (e.g., Smart, 1989; Wangmann, 2020). Such observations notwithstanding, efforts to criminalize coercive control have gained momentum and the purpose of this chapter is to consider these efforts and place them within the wider context of what Goodmark (2018) has coined as 'the criminalization thesis'.

Before moving into a more detailed consideration of these issues, it is important to note that historically, as Williams and Walklate (2020: 314) evidence,

> the wider civil changes in women's rights over access to divorces, custody over children and property being used more frequently than criminalisation, in attempts to improve the position of those women living with violence, at least those who were in a position to avail themselves of the opportunities that these civil changes afforded. What is more, it was these changes that women living with domestic violence themselves asked for time and again, in court, in public writings, and as they reached out to campaigners and lawmakers.

Indeed, there are several important issues embedded within this observation. First, the civil law and access to rights through civil and family law developments have had some significant import for women and children living with violence, especially in England and Wales but in other jurisdictions too. This is the case from the telling intervention made by Frances Power Cobbe in 1878 in her essay on 'Wife Torture' (an intervention which proved to be hugely influential in the 1878 amendment to the 1853 Matrimonial Proceedings Act which for the first time allowed women to separate from their husband on the grounds of cruelty, and enabled magistrates to issue protection orders to women whose husbands had been convicted of aggravated assault, see also D'Cruze, 1998) to the more recent 2020 judgement made in the Court of Appeal (Civil Division, England and Wales) in favour of a mother in relation to coercive control and the question of joint parental access to children. Second, historically, these civil changes impacted most on those who could make use of them. Third, it was these kinds of changes – relating to housing, custody, and divorce – that women asked for.

So, in terms of twentieth- and twenty-first-century pre-occupations with criminal law responses, as distinct from civil/family law responses, there are important messages to consider when policy responses designed to improve the lives of women and children are being proposed. Risking repetition, family law matters. Listening to women matters. Placing those lives within a wider socio-economic context, matters. These three fundamental themes frame the discussion which follows. However, while it is recognized that in some jurisdictions civil/family law responses do embrace the import of coercive control (notably in the State of Victoria, Australia), the focus of this chapter is primarily on the recourse to the *criminal* law as a response to coercive control. Before proceeding further, it will be of some value to set the desire to criminalize coercive control within already existing legal understandings of coercion in the criminal law, an issue which was also raised in Chapter 2.

What does coercion mean in criminal law?

The question of what coercion means in law and how it manifests itself in terms of co-offending behaviour, particularly coercion into crime, has been discussed in detail in Chapter 2. There is no intention to repeat those arguments here. Nevertheless, for the purposes of this discussion, and towards furthering our understanding of the potential space for the criminal law in relation to the concept of coercive control, it will be useful to reiterate some appreciation of how the law might construct coercion in the first instance.

As noted in earlier chapters, Brunk (1979) offers one analysis of coercion when used by legal practitioners in plea bargaining negotiations. This analysis draws attention to two interrelated questions: how the relationship between threat and coercion might be understood and what the conditions might be under which an individual 'chooses' a course of action. Both questions raise a more fundamental issue concerning what counts as voluntary or involuntary behaviour. For Brunck (1979) threat and coercion are separate and separable in law. Threats can be actionable in law though there is a requirement for corroborating evidence of a threat (a text message, a recorded telephone call, or a third-party witness). However, coercion is much more difficult to evidence in law. For coercion to be actionable in law, the context in which it takes place is key (Brunk, 1979). Herein lies an important link with Stark's (2007) conceptualization of coercive control: understanding the context in which a pattern of behaviour, and responses to that behaviour, occur. Brunk (1979) argues that when individuals make a choice, whatever the conditions of that choice might be, the choice making process assumes that there are a set of normal conditions against which the choice being made can be compared. Thus he goes on to state: '[t]o identify an intervention as coercive is to judge that it breaks with some common practice and/or violates a norm of morality, custom, or law' (Brunk, 1979: 538). So to establish coercion in law, it is necessary to make assumptions as to what might count as 'normal' to demonstrate that coercion (considered non-normal) has taken place. Logically this is a requirement in every situation in which an attempt to define coercion occurs.

While somewhat technical, Brunk's (1979) analysis serves as a useful reminder of the complexities that can occur when asserting coercion in law. It also serves as a reminder that such complexities also lie behind intimate relationships, in which what might constitute 'the normal' is also open to contestation (Renzetti, 1992). To be specific: the slippage between what might count as 'normal' in intimate relationships (in which wanting to know what each other is doing at any one point in time may be seen to be acceptable) to circumstances in which that 'wanting to know' becomes construed as surveillance and/or stalking, is one (obvious) complex and dynamic process. Moreover, as Hanna (2009: 1468) has pointed out,

> the law forces the question of illegal coercion into a yes or no answer. The line between free choice and coercion gets drawn some-where – and you are either coerced or not.

This observation points up very well the difficult relationship between understanding choice as voluntary and/or involuntary. So as discussed in Chapter 2, in cases of intimate partner homicide where a woman claims coercive control when killing her partner, evidence needs to be forthcoming as to the nature of that coercion and her subsequent ability to make choices. (Though as Chapter 2 also has illustrated, this is neither a simple nor straightforward process; see also Sheehy, 2014; Sheehy et al., 2012). In such circumstances, Midson (2016: 424) has suggested that

> [i]f the accused's choices are constrained or his or her will is over-borne by the will of another, the moral fault of the accused is, or at least may be, absent.

In other words, there is space for a potential defence case and/or plea of mitigation. Nevertheless dangers remain in translating this kind of appreciation of choice in a case of homicide. Arguably, in these circumstances, evidence for what Langer (1980) might say constitutes a 'choiceless choice' only becomes defensible when compared with the 'normality' of coercive control (qua Stark, 2007). Kuennan (2013: 6) expresses these dangers in the following way:

> This presumption of involuntariness, when coupled with the practical challenges of measuring the impact of coercion, poses

an enormous risk to victim autonomy. If a court substitutes its judgment for that of the victim's because it believes her to be coerced, and presumes that when she is coerced she cannot make an autonomous decision, it usurps control over a decision the victim would like to make for herself, thereby replicating the very dynamic it seeks to prevent. Instead of the batterer compelling the victim to do something she does not want, the court does. This is particularly problematic in cases involving domestic violence, in which an important element of responding to the problem is to restore a victim's fundamental rights of freedom, choice, and autonomy.

This is not a new problem. It is one generated as a result of investing energy in the criminal law as a response to domestic abuse (see, e.g., Mills, 1999; Bumiller, 2008) and hints at the ways in which the criminal law can, and does, act in the interests of the state rather than the interests of either individual women or women as a group. (This is developed more fully in Chapter 5). However, at this juncture it is important to note that the tensions commented on by Kuennan (2013) reflect one manifestation of the tensions confronting the law in endeavouring to reach a judgement in relation to interpersonal relationships. As she goes on to observe:

> In nonabusive relationships, it is a norm for women (and men) to make decisions about their intimate relationships based on love, particularly when deciding whether to end their intimate relationships. The question, then, is how do we as a society draw the line between abusive and nonabusive relationships so as to recognize staying for love as a legitimate reason to stay, rather than writing it off as maladaptive?
>
> (Kuennan, 2014: 993–994)

One way of making this distinction is to consider the ways in which fear influences decision-making, which a specific offence of coercive control may aim to capture. Nevertheless, as we will go on to discuss, drawing a line between abusive and non-abusive relationships poses problems not just for the law in theory but also for the law in practice. Such distinctions matter. Previous chapters have highlighted the many and varied ways in which women experience coercive control in intimate relationships. Translating those many and varied experiences into legal practice can be fraught with difficulties. Lewis and Greene (1978) have referred to this as the implementation gap. The question remains, however, why criminalize coercive control at all?

Why criminalize coercive control?

As earlier chapters in this book have documented, experiences of coercive and controlling behaviours are real and carry with them severe consequences for those on the receiving end of such behaviours. Recognizing the significance of these experiences is important for all those working within the field of domestic abuse. However, the extent to which the criminal law opens a 'space for action' (Sharp-Jeffs et al., 2018), particularly for victim-survivors, divides opinion. In one of the few studies asking women about their experiences and help-seeking behaviour in relation to coercive control, Boxall and Morgan (2021: 12) conclude:

> Importantly, women who had experienced coercive control were unlikely to seek help from formal or informal sources if they had not also experienced physical/sexual forms of abuse.

This comment alludes to some of the well-documented and problematic complexities for victim-survivors in relation to either what they might think is actionable and doable in law, the conditions under which they might choose the law as one way of seeking out a resolution to the violence in their lives, or indeed what they might want from criminal justice intervention. Tolmie (2018) reviews some arguments in favour of the criminalization of coercive control.

Tolmie (2018) suggests criminalizing coercive control places any physical violence experienced by victim-survivors in the context of their relationships and sensitizes police responses to non-violent and other forms of low-level offending. All of which may escalate to more overt physical abuse over time (see also Bettinson, 2016). Furthermore, greater awareness of the context of a case, should it be prosecuted, can help validate women's experiences of violence, and enable the court to make better-informed decisions, especially in relation to the disposition of the offender. This context could include psychological abuse, financial abuse, and abusive use of digital technologies. It would also include physical abuse but would not rely on this alone. An offence labelled in such a way can capture what has happened, especially over time, more effectively and can inform sentencing (see also Youngs, 2014). Douglas (2015) has also suggested that criminalizing coercive control has an educative function (as opposed to simply a symbolic function) and might help victims and the wider community recognize and make sense of their and other's experiences. Johnson et al. (2019) have also proffered the view that the law has power as a preventive strategy and if coercive control was recognized as a common feature of lethal relationships, it might prevent such deaths from happening (Johnson et al., 2019). However, in those jurisdictions in which specific offences of coercive control have been introduced, the jury is very much still out on whether such legislation can deliver on any of these presumed positive outcomes.

Not all jurisdictions have opted to respond to the increasing recognition and powerful presence of coercive control in abusive relationships with the introduction of specific offences. Following on from Walklate and Fitz-Gibbon (2019), it is possible to identify four different criminal justice strategies affording coercive control a presence in the justice process: as expert testimony, in constructing a specific defence for murder, as an adjunct to other offences, and as a stand-alone offence. While there is some overlap in the first two of these strategies, each of these will be discussed in turn.

Finding a place for coercive control in the criminal law

Expert testimony

The role of the expert in providing evidence as to the mental state and/ or capacity for any offender of any crime is well-established, though it is probably most contested in the context of murder/manslaughter. This is because decisions regarding the culpability of an offender are frequently related to the assignation of guilt and subsequent sentencing decisions. Expert testimony can then be significant in the deliberations of the court. Sheehy (2018) analyses the efforts made in the case of Teresa Craig in Canada to invoke coercive control in her defence for the murder of her partner. Evan Stark himself was the expert witness in this case and his presence as such was accepted by the court. Sheehy (2018) goes on to discuss the difficulties encountered and the questions posed for the court in this case in some detail. She concludes that the use of this kind of expert testimony (as opposed to that of a court recognized psychologist or psychiatrist) is likely to have limited success in Canada. Similarly, in the case of Sally Challen in England and Wales (discussed in more detail in Chapter 2), expert testimony relating to coercive control was also presented to the Court of Appeal by Evan Stark. A good deal of the media coverage surrounding Challen's appeal focused on this evidence and the role of the already existing offence of coercive control, introduced in England and Wales in 2015. However, as in Canada, the appeal judgement suggests that the evidence of coercive control, as presented to the court, was not as significant as might have been anticipated. Indeed, Lady Justice Hallett stated:

There might be those out there who think this appeal is all about coercive control but it's not … Primarily, it's about diagnosis of disorders that were undiagnosed at the time of the trial.

(cited in Curtis, 2019)

Thus, to date, expert testimony on its own, has had little success in securing positive outcomes from the court in cases of this kind. As Sheehy (2018) observes, to date the court seems to be far more comfortable with such experts presenting validated (in their view) evidence rooted in psychology and psychiatry as opposed to that rooted in understandings of interpersonal relationships.

Locating a space for expert testimony in relation to coercive control is pushed somewhat further by Douglas et al. (2021). In a detailed analysis they document the evidence needed to support a case of self-defence for murder when seen through the lens of social entrapment. This draws on the concept of coercive control, but in deploying the concept of social entrapment this work endeavours to deepen understandings of intimate partner violence by situating them squarely within the systemic as well as interpersonal power relationships experience as a result of structural and intersectional social inequality. (See Tolmie et al., 2018; FVDRC, 2016; Wilson et al., 2019). Using social entrapment as their frame Tolmie et al. (2021) make an evidenced and convincing case for expert testimony in cases where social entrapment can be documented and indicate the criteria such testimony would need to meet. They conclude by suggesting that in Australian jurisdictions:

While expert psychologists and psychiatrists have often been called in murder trials involving IPV, their evidence is focussed on the workings of the human mind. We suggest that expert testimony about understanding patterns of abusive behaviour in their social context would be appropriately provided by a social scientist or a social worker with expertise in this area.

(Tolmie et al., 2021: 354)

Clearly the debate surrounding the role of expert testimony in cases involving coercive control is ongoing and to date is unresolved. However, this debate surrounding the potential for a role for expert testimony in relation to coercive control slips, almost imperceptibly, into the more legally focused space of framing specific defence strategies for murder per se.

Specific defences in cases of murder (and other crimes)

Midson (2016) made some early observations reflecting on the possibilities of coercive control as a specific defence, particularly in cases of murder. She engaged in a comparative analysis of two cases and their associated judgements in New Zealand and explores the dual questions raised for the legal concepts of culpability and responsibility when viewed through the lens of coercive control. She reached the conclusion that,

> When victims of coercive control kill their abusers there is no 'malice aforethought' in the true sense of that phrase, despite the appearance of willed action. The act is not malicious or angry – it is a normative response to coercive conditions. On that basis, it is not just or fair to label these victims as 'murderers' or 'killers', even though the criminal justice system might rightly hold them responsible to some degree.
>
> (Midson, 2016: 1272)

In some respects, it was this tension between culpability and responsibility which was exposed in the appeal case of Sally Challen (referred to above). The undisputed presence of a weapon used by Challen to kill her partner constituted part of this problematic equation in this case.

Nevertheless, understanding the circumstances and the wider context under which such acts occur (like that of Challen) has been a fruitful route to re-orienting accepted interpretations of provocation as a partial defence for murder (as illustrated in the work of Fitz-Gibbon, 2014) and the Challen case, alongside the greater awareness of coercive control, may add to such re-orientations. More specifically the Prison Reform Trust of England and Wales has been involved in a campaign to encourage the recognition of coercive control as a route into all kinds of offending for women (see Chapter 2). They have also been vocal in seeking amendments to the 2021 Domestic Abuse Act (England and Wales), the success of which, at the time of writing, remains unclear.

Coercive control as an adjunct to already existing offences

In some jurisdictions, notably the United States, the push to criminalize coercive control has taken the form of adding this feature of domestic abuse to other behaviours already criminalized in the criminal code. Ortiz (2018), for example, makes the case that Tennessee, could adapt its law on false imprisonment to include a specific category defined as domestic false imprisonment. This might be categorized as:

A course of conduct intentional, knowing, reckless, or negligent repeated or continuing harassment, intimidation, exploitation, humiliation, isolation, and/or control, directed toward a person with whom the perpetrator has a personal connection, which interferes substantially with that person's liberty and autonomy.

(Ortiz, 2018: 707–709)

Following this line of argument in adapting already existing laws, Stansfield and Williams (2018) provide evidence between the use of threats to kill and the delivery of such threats. Based on this evidence, they conclude that:

The results consistently showed a robust empirical relation between perpetrators' death threats and subsequent escalation into nonfatal strangulation as a way of maintaining control through fear and intimidation.

(Stansfield and Williams, 2018: 14)

Thus an offence of non-fatal strangulation constitutes another way of ensuring the recognition of coercive control on the statute books. Offences of non-fatal strangulation exist in 47 jurisdictions in the United States (Theakston, 2019), have been introduced in New Zealand (NZ *Family Violence (Amendments) Act* 2018 s 189A), and have been introduced and/or debated in several Australian states and territories (Gotsis, 2018). This offence was also introduced into the 2021 Domestic Abuse Act (England and Wales).

Taking this route to securing coercive control on the statute books requires practitioners to embrace an understanding of it and its impact (see also Brennan et al., 2018). This is a process of change which has never been simple or straightforward. As was implied above, there is frequently a gap between the law in theory and the law in practice (Lewis and Greene, 1978). Such difficulties notwithstanding, other jurisdictions have taken the concept of coercive control further and have introduced specific legislation designed to criminalize the behaviour included within it. This strategy has provoked much debate and is reviewed in what follows.

A specific offence of coercive control

Over the last decade, introducing a specific offence of coercive control has either been implemented or considered across in a number of jurisdictions. For example, specific offences foregrounding coercive control have been differently introduced in England and Wales,

Scotland, the Republic of Ireland (Soliman, 2019), and have been considered in Canada, different states in Australia (Douglas, 2015), and debated in the United States (Tuerkheimer, 2007). Some of these interventions are gender-specific and some are not, some only apply to intimate partners and others include other family members. However, they all share the view that a new kind of criminal offence is needed to capture the pattern of abusive behaviours embedded in coercive control, that this constitutes a gap in the legal framework, and that such an intervention would fill this gap in an innovative way (Wiener, 2020). As will be developed, in some ways such interventions raise more questions than answers in respect of the efficacy of the criminal law as a response, for either violence against women generally or coercive control specifically.

One early legal intervention drawing on coercive control was the Tasmanian *Family Violence Act* 2004 (Tas). This legislation introduced two new offences: one of economic abuse and one of emotional abuse and intimidation. Both offences were defined in relation to an ongoing course of conduct, though to date neither has secured many prosecutions. McMahon and McGorrery (2016) have suggested several reasons for this but point primarily to limitations inherent in the formulation of the law itself. Their observations echo some of the early commentary associated with the specific offence of coercive control introduced in England and Wales in December 2015, amended in the 2021 legislation and discussed in detail in Chapter 1. The definition in this legislation explicitly draws on the work of Stark (2007) except regarding the question of gender. The legislation, both in 2015 and 2021, is framed in gender-neutral terms. In contrast, the Scottish legislation introduced in 2018, recognizes the gendered pattern of domestic abuse and also includes ex-partners within its remit (Domestic Abuse (Scotland) Act, 2018; see further Burman and Brooks-Hay, 2018; Stark and Hester, 2019). (The 2021 legislation in England Wales now also includes ex-partners). However, Scottish legislation has come to be referred to as the 'gold standard' (Scott, 2020) in terms of its appropriateness and efficacy as a legal response. Yet, the extent to which either pieces of legislation have been taken up and acted upon within the criminal justice process since their introduction is still under scrutiny.

Statistics for the year ending March 2019 indicate a fourfold increase in cases of coercive control receiving a first hearing in a magistrate's court (from 309 year ending March 2017 to 1177 year ending March 2019) with 308 convictions in which coercive control was the principal offence being tried in the year ending December 2018 (Office of National Statistics, 2019). Given that the police recorded 1.3 million domestic abuse related crimes in the year ending March 2019 and in that same year the Crime Survey for England and Wales estimated that 2.4 million people experienced domestic abuse, these figures highlight the ongoing relatively low usage of the offence. In a detailed statistical and evidenced review of the coercive control legislation (Home Office, 2021), one conclusion there points out:

> There is currently a lack of robust data on CCB prevalence, making it difficult to measure how effective the offence has been at capturing CCB offending. There is no common statistical definition of CCB used across survey data, administrative data collected by third-sector organisations and research data, making it difficult to compare prevalence and characteristics of CCB across different sources.

In a recent empirical study on the implementation of the 2015 legislation based on Freedom of Information requests from police forces in England and Wales, Brennan and Myhill (2021: 14) found that:

> the rate of charge or summons for perpetrators of controlling or coercive behaviour offences was half that for other domestic abuse offences, and the likelihood that a case would be discontinued because of evidential difficulties was over 50% more likely than for other domestic abuse offences.

Of course, some of the issues found in this study are pertinent to criminal justice responses in all cases of domestic abuse and lack of comparable data does make efficacy claims on behalf of specific legislation more difficult. However, as is developed below, some work has focused on such claims and the associated problems of implementation. (At this juncture, it is worth noting that at the time of writing there are no official comparable figures from Scotland where the legislation did not come into effect until April 2019.)

In terms of evaluation of the efficacy of the 2015 legislation, while McGorrery and McMahon (2019) make some positive claims in this regard, it is important to note that their analysis is based on press coverage of cases. This is limited as a source of data. Nevertheless, what has been evidenced is the difficulties associated with translating this law into practice. For example, data reported by the Bureau of Investigative Journalism (McClenaghan and Boutaud, 2017) illustrated that the initial take up of this legislation was patchy and suggested varied levels of implementation in different police forces, evidencing issues with 'justice by geography'. Early evaluations also pointed to problems for front-line police officers in 'seeing' coercive control (Wiener, 2017); in practitioner understandings of coercive control more generally (Robinson et al., 2018a; Brennan et al., 2018); and problems associated with evidencing this offence (Bishop and Bettinson, 2018). In a study analysing police responses to coercive control in partnership with a police force based in the North of England, Barlow et al. (2020) identified that less than 1% of all domestic abuse offences were recorded as coercive control (in the year 2016–2017). This work engaged in both quantitative and qualitative analyses, paying particular attention to those cases in which it was possible to identify patterns of abuse. Based on this work, this research suggests police officers may be missing key opportunities for identifying such abuse with the tendency to focus on isolated incidents of abuse proving to be persistent. Evidential opportunities were often missed, including not fully investigating evidence of coercive control disclosed in victim witness statements (such as behaviours being disclosed and not followed up by police officers), failure to seek third party witness statements, and failing to capture effectively the victim's initial account or using body-worn cameras as a source of evidence.

The focus on physical violence when responding to domestic abuse also influenced police officers' assessment of risk and likelihood of arrest in such cases. Tolmie (2018) suggested that the coercive control offence may only lead to successful charges in cases where physical violence is present, consequently minimizing the nature of intimate partner violence in non-physical contexts. The empirical work by Barlow et al. (2020) supports this view with many of the (few) successful prosecutions in this research featuring evidence of physical violence. This echoes the earlier findings of Robinson et al. (2018b) which pointed to the 'small constellation of risk factors' embraced by police officers in their decision-making in relation to domestic abuse and is also supportive of the observations made by Tolmie (2018) and the Home Office (2021) review of this offence.

The emphasis on physical violence as a risk factor is hardly surprising since risk assessment tools are designed to assess what is measurable and actionable. Neither of these readily translate into assessing the kinds of risks present in a pattern or web of abusive behaviour. Nevertheless, there is some evidence to support the view that training interventions for police officers can both improve their understanding of coercive control and procedures for evidencing it in conjunction with the adoption of a positive stance towards domestic abuse more generally (Brennan et al., 2021). However, what might be seen as a positive intervention on the part of the police also needs to be viewed in the same light by other criminal justice professionals and partner agencies, as well as being seen to be positive by victim-survivors themselves. This issue is explained later in this chapter.

To summarize, the problems so far identified with a recourse to the criminal law generally and the development of specific offences of coercive control particularly, especially in relation to their implementation, are not new to the field of domestic abuse. There are, and have been historically, difficulties in shifting the criminal justice gaze away from incidents to processes. This is required for the recognition of coercive control (Kelly and Westmarland, 2016). This re-orientation in approach also applies to the problems of evidencing coercion (Bishop and Bettinson, 2018; Brennan and Myhill, 2021). Moreover, it has been well-documented that the law is a blunt instrument in affording change to the wider social practices of violence rooted in gender inequality (see inter alia Smart, 1989; Goodmark, 2018). Tolmie (2018) provides a substantial summary of the arguments both for and against using the law in this way, with Douglas (2018) suggesting that the law itself can act as a site of abuse, adding to and exacerbating the list of abuses women already experience in their relationship. Walklate et al. (2018) offer a more detailed analysis of the specific problems associated with this particular offence, while Burman and Brooks-Hay (2018: 78) conclude their analysis of what was then the prospective Scottish legislation by stating:

> Decades of policy and legislative reform of the criminal justice response to other forms of violence against women leave us somewhat pessimistic that the introduction of this new offence within Scotland's adversarial context, which sustains forms of legal practice known to effectively undermine the spirit of any well-intentioned legislation, will fully achieve its bold ambitions … Legislative change cannot on its own lead to improvements. Whatever laws we have will be only as effective as those who enforce, prosecute and apply them. Improving these practices – through education, training and embedding best practice and domestic abuse expertise – is likely to be more effective than the creation of new offences alone.

As already indicated, Burman and Brooks-Hay (2018) are articulating a long-standing dilemma within this field. However, it is important to add that the recourse to the law in the context of this specific offence, also fails to recognize three issues: the law itself as coercive and controlling (Douglas, 2018); the problems of operationalizing coercion as it already exists within legal discourse (Brunk, 1979); and the associated problems of (in)voluntariness (Kuennan, 2014). In addition, it is possible to add to this list the emergent issue of misrecognizing the victim as the principal offender (see inter alia Nancarrow, 2019; Reeves, 2021). All these failures add to the fundamental question asked by Crossman and Hardesty (2018: 196): 'what makes control coercive?' Perhaps expressing this question in a slightly different way, there are clearly difficulties in evidencing the extent to which the recourse to the criminal law achieves either improved safety outcomes for women (especially women who are particularly marginalized from the criminal justice process) and/or enhances perpetrator accountability. In the light of these questions, it will be useful to push the question of victim-survivor voices in relation to criminal justice in general and the criminalization of coercive control particularly, a little further.

Finding a space for victim-survivor experiences

In some ways the speed with which coercive control as a specific offence has grasped policy imaginations reflects that which Goodmark (2015) has called 'exporting without a licence' and that which Walklate and Fitz-Gibbon (2019) have called 'coercive control creep'. This offence creep, however, contains within it a number of problematic assumptions when seen through the eyes of what is known about victim-survivors' embrace of criminal justice processes.

The offence of coercive control relies on the willingness of victims to engage in the legal and criminal justice process to secure a successful prosecution. It is important to acknowledge that frequently there is less physical evidence in coercive control cases when compared with other domestic abuse related offences such as actual bodily harm or criminal damage. This means that victim testimony can be vital in securing a charge, the option of evidence-led prosecutions notwithstanding. Stark's (2007) emphasis on coercive control as a 'liberty crime' is rooted in an assumption that women would want, or feel able, to provide a detailed narrative of their experience in court or would trust another to do so on their behalf. Victim-survivor reluctance to engage with criminal justice is well-documented and is particularly pertinent when viewed through the lens of structural inequalities such as race, ethnicity, class, disability, and Indigenous status (Nancarrow, 2019). Reflecting on the work discussed in Chapter 2, it is important to note that women as offenders coerced into crime are also unlikely to engage in the criminal justice process concerning their experiences of victimization consequent to their own experiences of criminalization and the coercive nature of the system itself (Barlow, 2019). It is also the case that victims of coercive control can experience further abuse and the exertion of power and control by their abusers when they attempt to prosecute (Douglas, 2015).

Coercive control is highly complex with perpetrators often able to create a false reality of 'what is actually going on here'; a reality which in turn can become internalized by victim-survivors. This renders engagement within the criminal justice process challenging for them, and the response of criminal justice professionals, including prosecutors and judges, central to the success or otherwise of any prosecution. As Tolmie (2018) points out, assuming victim-survivors can address bad relationships by 'choosing' to leave, or they can keep themselves and their children safe by contacting the police or getting a protection order, is hugely problematic. These assumptions also put the burden of responsibility for addressing the perpetrator's behaviour onto the victim. Responsibilizing the victim-survivor in this way constitutes a danger especially when they have children (see inter alia Meyer, 2011). Frequently women believe what their partners have told them about their ability as mothers and the likelihood of them losing access to their children should they report their partner for abusive behaviour. Such fears become more acute the more marginalized the woman is. For example, for women living with disability the 'fear of retribution or a loss of support' can be heightened if the perpetrator they report is also their carer (Royal Commission into Family Violence (RCFV), 2016: 31, 183; McCulloch et al., 2020). Similarly, issues in relation to reporting behaviour and engagement in the criminal justice system can be acute for Indigenous women. For example, Wilson (2017: 288) reports that:

> The under-reporting of family violence for indigenous peoples is a concern made worse by structural discrimination, fear of being excluded from their community, fears about consequences for the offender, lack of access to services due to rurality and remoteness, and encountering culturally inappropriate responses.

These silencing processes add to women 'Feeling unsafe within one's family and within a system designed to provide helping services can place indigenous women and children at greater risk of serious injury and death' (Wilson, 2017: 289).

Some of these same issues also apply to those men who have experienced coercive control and while it is widely accepted that coercive control is a gendered phenomenon, this does not mean it is only done by men to women. As Chapter 3 has documented, men can be subjected to coercive control too and while their experiences may take on a different shape and form and are most frequently expressed in terms of access to children, they too can feel unheard in the criminal justice process. These 'contextual complexities' (Wilson, 2017) not only raise fundamental questions about the appropriateness of criminal justice responses in general, but also about understandings of coercive control in particular. In the case of the latter, the coercive and controlling behaviour of a partner may be seen as more tolerable than the coercive and controlling responses of the state and its authorities (Wilson, 2020; see also Nancarrow, 2019). Such contextual and structural complexities are also evident for migrant women, women whose visa status may be temporary (Maher and Segrave, 2018), and women for whom offending family honour may be a more traumatic prospect than living with the violence in their lives (Gill and Harrison, 2016).

These observations provide some insight into the complexity of criminalization and in using the law as an avenue for innovation and/ or as a mechanism for changing such complexities. In sum, for those women for whom the state and/or their family are feared more than their partner, to engage 'successfully' with criminal justice they must demonstrate that they are blameless victims. The reality is that the state finds it much easier to construct these and other women as dual offenders than it does to readily accept their status as a victim-survivor (see, for example, Reeves and Meyer, 2021, Stubbs and Wangmann, 2015). With all of this in mind, the criminalization of coercive control may work for some women, but it will not work for all and indeed it may further marginalize others. In practice criminalization is not a quick fix policy option.

The debate generated around the introduction of coercive control as a specific offence discussed above is in many ways a manifestation of a deeper problem which has plagued those committed to changing policy responses to violence against women since the 1970s. This problem is: how and under what conditions might a criminal justice response to such violence(s) be an effective one? Goodmark (2018) refers to this problem as the 'criminalization thesis'.

The criminalization thesis

The criminalization thesis grew in prominence during the 1980s, particularly in the United States and spread soon after to other parts of the Anglo-speaking world. During the late 1970s and 1980s, the voices demanding tougher responses to crime more generally became aligned with feminist voices campaigning for all violence(s) against women to be taken more seriously, particularly within the criminal justice system.

As recognition of, and concern about, violence against women became more prominent, the policy responses developed in response to these concerns became marked by a recourse to the law. (See, inter alia, Walklate, 2008; Smart, 1989). It is important to note that not all feminist voices spoke as one in relation to this. Some pointed to the fact than changing the law and its practice was only one piece of the puzzle (see, e.g., Wilson, 1983) and Goodmark's (2018) analysis does point to the myriad ways in which focusing attention on criminal justice has been beneficial for some women. However, as Goodmark (2018) goes on to outline, and has been intimated above, these same practices do not impact on all women (and some men) in the same way. Importantly, as Stubbs and Wangmann (2015) evidence, the different legal domains women are exposed to when their experiences of violence come to the attention of the authorities, requires them to perform themselves differently (to fit with the expectations of these different authorities as legitimate and/or blameless victims) to secure legal redress and safety for themselves and their children (see also McCulloch et al., 2020; Meyer, 2011). At the same time Goodmark (2018) has argued that many of the policies marked by criminalization have added to the hyper-incarceration of men of colour (especially in the United States) and have committed police and criminal justice resources in ways in which it is difficult to see what good effect they might have had (see also Goodmark, 2020).

Goodmark (2018) is clearly commenting on the impact that this move towards criminalization has had in the United States, ultimately asking the question: does criminalization deter? Despite the US orientation of her analysis, the issues raised in her work are pertinent to the recurring recourse to law found in other jurisdictions across the global north and south. While this work proffers some interesting questions around global convergence in relation to criminalization, significant institutional/local differences remain (see Carrington et al., 2018). Echoing observations made earlier in this chapter; Lacey (2016) observes that the law in action is not the same as the law in books (as the problems of implementing coercive control laws referred to above illustrate). Thus a deeper analysis of the problems and possibilities of criminalization is called for. Put simply, in searching for that deeper analysis criminalization is rendered more complex. This serves to remind us that the criminal law, in the creation of the legal subjects of law (complainants and defendants), is intimately connected with understandings of responsibility (in law) and the construction of the responsible subject (of law). This subject, as Lacey (2013) reminds us, is gendered. Thus in law, who did what to whom and why, is interconnected and gendered. These are not new observations, but an understanding of their import is often absent from the desire to expand the remit of the criminal law to capture coercive and controlling behaviours. The failure to recognize the silent but pervasive influence of these issues in the recourse to law is telling and important for (at least) two reasons. It brings more clearly into view the questions of who the subject of criminalization is and whose interests are served in the construction of this subject. This requires further explication and is discussed in the chapter that follows.

Concluding thoughts

This chapter has explored the increasing policy interest in, and focus on, what is known about the impact of coercive control on those subjected to it and the role of the criminal law. The chapter has noted the different ways in which different criminal justice agendas have embraced the need for this kind of response and reviewed the problems and possibilities associated with it. Importantly this discussion has considered this desire for criminalization in the context of not only the increasing awareness of coercive control itself, but also in the context of thinking about what coercion might mean in law and the historical embrace of criminal law (discussed here in reference to Goodmark's delineation of the criminalization thesis) and its unintended consequences. Reflecting on those unintended consequences has led to a further consideration of the under-explored question of the extent to which the criminalization of coercive control meets the requirement of meeting women's (and children's) desire for safety. This point is perhaps worth developing further.

The wider reluctance of women to engage in the criminal justice process more generally is not only well-documented but also needs to be a central concern for the debates discussed here. To date, the voices of advocates notwithstanding, there is little evidence available to be able to make decision on the relationship between rendering coercive control illegal and resultant improved safety for women (and children). Recognizing this as a central issue provokes the need to unpack a range of further questions in relation to this agenda, some of which have been alluded to in the discussion above. Put simply, for the purposes of this conclusion, if improving women's (and children's) safety is of central concern then consideration needs to be given to several issues. One question which remains is the extent to which criminalizing coercive control enhances women's safety and if it does not, what else needs to be in place to ensure that it does. This might lead to a more holistic approach to understanding the criminal justice system as a system and the need then, for example, for common understandings of risk and risk assessment which put women's voices at the centre (Barlow and Walklate, 2021), and for robust and commonly grounded information sharing systems that do not put women's and children's interests at odds with one other (Hester's [2011] 'three planets' model is of relevance here). In the absence of asking these questions, the elephant in the room might be the question: whose interests are being served in the criminalization of coercive control? At this juncture, it is possible to offer some insight and a partial answer to this question.

Criminalizing coercive control certainly serves the interests of the state in appearing to be 'doing something' about violence against women. However, more concerningly, it also potentially ensures the ongoing marginalization of Indigenous women, ethnic minority women, women living with disability and so on as some of the work referenced in the discussion above articulates. It does this primarily by leaving the man of the law invisible (Naffine, 2019) in whose presence women are required ever to be blameless victims (Fitz-Gibbon and Walklate, 2021). These are the questions to be developed further in the chapter that follows.

References

Barlow C (2019) Coercion and women co-offenders: A gendered pathway into crime. Bristol: Bristol University Press.

Barlow C, Johnson J, Walklate S and Humphreys L (2020) Putting coercive control into practice: Problems and possibilities. *The British Journal of Criminology 60*(1): 160–179.

Barlow C and Walklate S (2021) Gender, risk assessment and coercive control: Contradictions in terms?, *The British Journal of Criminology 61*(4): 887–904, https://doi.org/10.1093/bjc/azaa104

Bettinson V (2016) Criminalising coercive control in domestic violence cases: Should Scotland follow the path of England and Wales? *Criminal Law Review 3*: 165–180.

Bishop C and Bettinson V (2018) Evidencing domestic violence, including behaviour that falls under the new offence of 'controlling or coercive behaviour'. *The International Journal of Evidence and Proof 22*(1): 3–29. https://doi.org/10.1177%2F1365712717725535

Boxall H and Morgan A (2021) Experiences of coercive control among Australian women. *Australian Institute of Criminology, Statistical Bulletin 30*. Aic.gov.au

Bumiller K (2008) *In an abusive state.* Durham, NC: Duke University Press.

Burman M and Brooks-Hay O (2018) Aligning policy and law? The creation of a domestic abuse offence incorporating coercive control. *Criminology and Criminal Justice 18*(1): 67–83. https://doi.org/10.1177%2F1748895817752223

Brennan IR, Burton V, Gormally S and O'Leary N (2018) Service provider difficulties in operationalizing coercive control. *Violence against Women 25*(6): 635–653. https://doi.org/10.1177%2F1077801218797478

Brennan I, Myhill A, Tagliaferri G and Tapley J (2021) Policing a new domestic abuse crime: effects of force-wide training on arrests for coercive control, Policing and Society, 31:10, 1153–1167, DOI: 10.1080/10439463.2020.1862838

Brennan IR and Myhill A (2021) Coercive control: Patterns in crimes, arrests and outcomes for a new domestic abuse offence, *The British Journal of Criminology*; azab072, https://doi.org/10.1093/bjc/azab072

Brunk GG (1979) The problem of voluntariness and coercion in the negotiated plea. *Law and Society Review 13*(2): 527–553. doi: 10.2307/3053267.

Carrington K, Hogg R, Scott J and Sozzo M (Eds.) (2018) *The Palgrave handbook of criminology and the global south.* London: Palgrave.

Crossman K and Hardesty J (2018) Placing coercive control at the center: What are the processes of coercive control and what makes control coercive? *Psychology of Violence 8*(2): 196–206. https://psycnet.apa.org/doi/10.1037/vio0000094

Curtis J (2019) Woman, 65, who killed her husband with a hammer after decades of abuse weeps in court as she has her 2011 murder conviction overturned in watershed moment for 'coercive control' law. *Daily Mail,* 1 March. Available at www.dailymail.co.uk/news/article-6756499/Wife-65-killed-husband-hammer-freed.html (accessed 1 March 2019)

D'Cruze S (1998) *Crimes of outrage: Sex, violence and Victorian working women.* London: UCL Press.

Douglas H (2015) Do we need a specific domestic violence offence? *Melbourne University Law Review 39*(2): 434–471.

Douglas H (2018) Legal systems abuse and coercive control. *Criminology and Criminal Justice 18*(1): 84–99.

Douglas H, Tarrant S and Tolmie J (2021) Social entrapment evidence: Understanding its role in self-defence cases involving intimate partner violence *UNSW Law Journal 44*(1): 324–354.

Family Violence Death Review Committee (FVDRC) (2016) Fifth report: January 2014 to December 2015. Wellington: Family Violence Death Review Committee.

Fitz-Gibbon K (2014) *Homicide law reform, gender and the provocation defence: A comparative perspective.* London: Palgrave-MacMillan.

Gill AK and Harrison K (2016) Police responses to intimate partner sexual violence in South Asian communities. *Policing 10*(4): 446–455. https://doi.org/10.1093/police/paw027

Goodmark L (2015) Exporting without license: The American attempt to end intimate partner abuse worldwide. In Goel R and Goodmark L (Eds.) *Comparative perspectives on gender violence: Lessons from efforts worldwide* (pp. 3–14). Oxford: Oxford University Press.

Goodmark L (2018) *Decriminalizing domestic violence: A balanced policy approach to intimate partner violence.* Berkeley, CA: University of California Press.

Goodmark L (2020) Reimagining VAWA: Why criminalization is a failed policy and what a non-carceral VAWA could look like. *Violence against Women* 27(1): 84–101. https://doi.org/10.1177/1077801220949686

Gotsis T (2018) NSW's strangulation offence: Time for further reform? *NSW Parliamentary Research Service Issues Backgrounder, Number 3*. Sydney: Parliamentary Library.

Hanna C (2009) The paradox of progress: Translating Evan Stark's coercive control into legal doctrine for abused women. *Violence against Women* 15(12): 1458–1476.

Hester M (2011) The three planet model: Towards an understanding of contradictions in approaches to women and children's safety in contexts of domestic violence. *The British Journal of Social Work 41*(5): 837–853, https://doi.org/10.1093/bjsw/bcr095

Home Office (2021) *Review of the controlling or coercive behaviour offence.* London: Home Office.

Johnson H, Eriksson L, Mazerolle P and Wortley R (2019) Intimate femicide: The role of coercive control. *Feminist Criminology 14*(1): 3–23. http://doi.org/10.1177/1557085117701574

Kelly L and Westmarland N (2016) Naming and defining 'domestic violence': Lessons from research with violent men. *Feminist Review 112*(1): 113–127.

Kuennan T (2013) Analyzing the impact of coercion on domestic violence victims: How much is too much? *Berkeley Journal of Gender, Law and Justice* 22(1): 2–30.

Kuennan T (2014) Love matters. *Arizona Law Review 56*(4): 977–1015.

Langer L (1980) The dilemma of choice in the deathcamps. *Centerpoint 4*(Fall): 222–231.

Lewis R and Greene JR (1978) Implementation evaluation: A future direction in project evaluation. *Journal of Criminal Justice 6*(2): 167–176.

Lewis R et al. (2001) Law's progressive potential: The value of engagement with the law for domestic violence, *Social and Legal Studies 10*(1): 105–130. doi: 10.1177/a017834. https://doi.org/10.1057/fr.2015.52

McClenaghan M and Boutaud C (2017) Questions raised over patchy take-up of domestic violence law. *The Bureau of Investigative Journalism*, 24 November. Available at www.thebureauinvestigates.com/stories/2017-11-24/coercive-control-concerns (accessed 11 September 2019).

Lacey N (2013) The rule of law and the political economy of criminalisation: An agenda for research. *Punishment and Society 15*(4): 349–366. https://doi.org/10.1177/1462474513500619

Lacey N (2016) *In search of criminal responsibility.* Oxford: Oxford University Press.

Maher J and Segrave M (2018) Family violence risk, migration status and 'vulnerability': Hearing the voices of immigrant women. *Journal of Gender Based Violence 2*(3): 503–518. https://doi.org/10.1332/239868018X15375304047178

McCulloch J, Maher J, Walklate S, McGowan J, Fitz-Gibbon K (2020) Justice perspectives of women with disability: An Australian story. *International Review of Victimology*. https://doi.org/10.1177/0269758020906270

McGorrery P and McMahon M (2019) Prosecuting controlling or coercive behaviour in England and Wales: Media reports of a novel offence. *Criminology and Criminal Justice 21*(4): 566–584. https://doi.org/10.1177/1748895819880947

McMahon M and McGorrery P (2016) Criminalising emotional abuse, intimidation and economic abuse in the context of family violence: The Tasmanian experience. *University of Tasmania Law Review 35*(2): 1–22.

Meyer S (2011) Seeking help for intimate partner violence: Victims' experiences when approaching the criminal justice system for IPV-related support and protection in an Australian jurisdiction. *Feminist Criminology 6*(4): 268–290. https://doi.org/10.1177/1557085111414860

Midson B (2016) Coercive control and criminal responsibility: Victims who kill their abusers. *Criminal Law Forum 27*(4): 417–442. https://doi.org/10.1007/s10609-016-9292-5

Mills L (1999) Killing her softly: Intimate abuse and the violence of state intervention. *Harvard Law Review 113*(2): 550–613. https://doi.org/10.2307/1342332

Naffine N (2019) *Criminal law and the man problem.* London: Hart Publishing.

Nancarrow H (2019) *Unintended consequences of domestic violence law: Gendered aspirations and racialised realities.* Hampshire: Palgrave MacMillan.

Office of National Statistics (2019) *Domestic Abuse Prevalence and Trends, England and Wales: Year Ending March 2019.* https://www.ons.gov.uk/peoplepopulationandcommunity/crimeandjustice/articles/domesticabuseprevalenceandtrendsenglandandwales/yearendingmarch2019

Ortiz AM (2018) Invisible bars: Adapting the crime of false imprisonment to better address coercive control and domestic violence in Tennessee. *Vanderbilt Law Review 71*: 682–715.

Reeves E (2021) 'I'm not at all protected and I think other women should know that, that they're not protected either': Victim–survivors' experiences of 'misidentification' in Victoria's family violence system. *International Journal for Crime, Justice and Social Democracy.* Advance online publication. https://doi.org/10.5204/ijcjsd.1992

Reeves E and Meyer S (2021) Marginalized women, domestic, and family violence reforms and their unintended consequences. In Erez E and Ibarral P (Eds.) *Oxford encyclopedia of international criminology.* New York and Oxford: Oxford University Press.

Renzetti C (1992) *Violent betrayal: Partner abuse in lesbian relationships.* Newbury Park, CA: Sage.

Robinson AL, Myhill A and Wire J (2018a) Practitioner (mis)understandings of coercive control in England and Wales. *Criminology and Criminal Justice 18*(1): 29–49. https://doi.org/10.1177%2F1748895817728381

Robinson, AL, Pinchevsky G and Guthrie J (2018b) A small constellation: Risk factors informing police perceptions of domestic abuse. *Policing and Society 28*(2): 189–204. https://doi.org/10.1080/10439463.2016.1151881

Royal Commission into Family Violence (2016) *Report and recommendations*. Melbourne: Royal Commission into Family Violence (Victoria).

Scott M (2020) The making of the new 'gold standard': The Domestic Abuse (Scotland) Act 2018. In McMahon M and McGorrery P (Eds.) *Criminalising coercive control: Family violence and the criminal law* (pp. 176–194). Singapore: Springer.

Sharp-Jeffs N, Kelly L and Klein R (2018) Long journeys toward freedom: The relationship between coercive control and space for action – measurement and emerging evidence. *Violence against Women 24*(2): 163–185. doi: 10.1177/1077801216686199.

Sheehy E, Stubbs J and Tolmie J (2012) Battered women charged with homicide in Australia, Canada and New Zealand: How do they fare? *Australian and New Zealand Journal of Criminology 45*(3): 383–399.

Sheehy E (2014) *Defending battered women on trial: Lessons from the transcripts*. Vancouver: University of British Columbia Press.

Sheehy E (2018) Expert evidence on coercive control in support of self-defence: The trial of Teresa Craig. *Criminology and Criminal Justice 18*(1): 100–114. https://doi.org/10.1177%2F1748895817733524

Sheley Erin L (2020) Criminalizing coercive control within the limits of due process. 11 February, *Duke Law Journal,* Forthcoming, Available at SSRN: https://ssrn.com/abstract=3536313

Smart C (1989) *Feminism and the power of law*. London: Routledge.

Soliman F (2019) The criminalisation of coercive control. Research and Information Service Research Paper NIAR 103-2019.

Stansfield R and Williams KR (2018) Coercive control between intimate partners: An application to nonfatal strangulation. *Journal of Interpersonal Violence 36*(9–10): NP5105–NP5124. https://doi.org/10.1177%2F0886260518795175

Stark E (2007) *Coercive control: How men entrap women in personal life*. Oxford: Oxford University Press.

Stark E and Hester M (2019) Coercive control: Update and review. *Violence against Women 25*(1): 81–104. https://doi.org/10.1177%2F1077801218816191

Stubbs J and Wangmann JM (2015) Competing conceptions of victims of domestic violence within legal processes. In Wilson D and Ross S (Eds.) *Crime, victims and policy*. (pp. 107–132). Basingstoke: Palgrave Macmillan. http://dx.doi.org/10.2139/ssrn.2627260

Theakston S (2019) 'Horrific act.' Why Kentucky needs to make non-fatal strangulation a felony. *Lexington Herald Leader*, 11 February. Available at www.kentucky.com/opinion/op-ed/article226087915.html (accessed 11 September 2019).

Tolmie J (2018) Coercive control: To criminalize or not to criminalize? Criminology and *Criminal Justice 18*(1): 50–66. https://doi.org/10.1177%2F1748895817746712

Tolmie J, Smith R, Short J, Wilson D and Sach J (2018) Social entrapment: A realistic understanding of the criminal offending of primary victims of intimate partner violence. *New Zealand Law Review* 2018(2): 181–217.

Tuerkheimer D (2007) Renewing the call to criminalize domestic violence: An assessment three years later. *George Washington Law Review 75*: 101–114.

Walklate S (2008) What is to be done about violence against women? *British Journal of Criminology 48*(1): 39–54. https://doi.org/10.1093/bjc/azm050

Walklate S, Fitz-Gibbon K and McCulloch J (2018) Is more law the answer? Seeking justice for victims of intimate partner violence through the reform of legal categories. *Criminology and Criminal Justice 18*(1): 115–131. https://doi.org/10.1177/1748895817728561

Walklate S and Fitz-Gibbon K (2019) The criminalisation of coercive control: The power of law? *International Journal for Crime, Justice and Social Democracy 8*(4): 94–108. https://doi.org/10.5204/ijcjsd.v8i4.1205

Walklate S and Fitz-Gibbon K (2021) Why criminalise coercive control? The complicity of the criminal law in punishing women through furthering the power of the state. *International Journal for Crime, Justice and Social Democracy*. Advance online publication. https://doi.org/10.5204/ijcjsd.1829

Wangmann, J (2020) Coercive control as the context for intimate partner violence: The challenge for the legal system. In McMahon M and McGorrery P (Eds.) *Criminalising coercive control*, (pp. 219–242). Singapore: Springer Nature. https://doi.org/10.1007/978-981-15-0653-6_11

Wiener C (2017) Seeing what is 'invisible in plain sight': Policing coercive control. *The Howard Journal of Crime and Justice 56*(4): 500–515. https://doi.org/10.1111/hojo.12227

Williams L and Walklate S (2020) Policy responses to domestic violence, the criminalisation thesis and 'learning from history'. *The Howard Journal of Crime and Justice 59*: 305–316. https://doi.org/10.1111/hojo.12378

Wilson D (2017) Indigenous populations and the domestic homicide review process. In Dawson M (Ed.) *Domestic homicides and death reviews* (pp. 287–316). London: Palgrave-Macmillan.

Wilson D (2020) *Colonisation, race and coercive control*. Paper presented at Criminalizing Coercive Control Webinar, de Montford University, 30–31 July 2020.

Wilson D, Mikahere-Hall A, Sherwood J, Cootes K and Jackson D (2019) *E Tū Wāhine, E Tū Whānau: Wāhine Māori keeping safe in unsafe relationships*. Auckland, NZ: Taupua Waiora Māori Research Centre.

Wilson E (1983) *What is to be done about violence against women?* Harmondsworth: Penguin.

Youngs J (2014) Domestic violence and criminal law: Reconceptualising reform. *Journal of Criminal Law 79*(1): 55–70. https://doi.org/10.1177/0022018314566746

5 Coercive control, the man of law, and the role of the state

Introduction

The previous chapter posited that criminalizing coercive control as a feature of interpersonal relationships certainly serves the interests of advocates, politicians, and policy-makers in appearing to be 'doing something' about violence against women. However, and arguably more concerningly, this drive to 'do something' carries with it unintended consequences. This desire can, and does, ensure the ongoing marginalization of Indigenous women, ethnic minority women, women living with disability, among others. These groups' experiences of intimate partner abuse and abuse by the state have been rather invisible in the moves towards criminalizing coercive control. There is, of course, a good deal of evidence available, as some of the work referenced in the previous chapter testifies to, addressing what the experiences and concerns of these groups look like. Moreover, it is the case that once these voices and concerns are put at the centre of the desire to 'do something', the debate to criminalize coercive control faces a fundamental problem. That problem, expressed in simple terms, is the problem of the man of law. This phrase is a short-hand way of expressing the ways in which, the presumed subject of law (the person for, by, and with whom law is constituted and in whose interests it operates) is left invisible (Naffine, 2019). Left in the shadow of this subject of law, women are required forever to be blameless victims (Walklate and Fitz-Gibbon, 2021). The purpose of this chapter is to excavate the presence of the man of law and to consider its implications for the further development of policy responses to coercive control.

DOI: 10.4324/9781003019114-5

Coercive control, the law, and unintended consequences

Following Balfour (2021), this chapter is concerned with the complex interplay between moves to criminalize ever more features of the dynamics of the wide range of violence(s) that can, and do, exist in interpersonal and intimate relationships, and the wider neo-liberal thrust given to governing through crime (Garland, 2001; Simon, 2006). To be clear, and as has been noted in the different chapters of this book, coercive control can, and does, have deleterious consequences for those subjected to it. Moreover, for some women (and men) some of the time the recourse to the criminal law can, and does, offer them a way out of relationships of this kind. However, the point has also been made in those same preceding chapters, that the law is a very blunt instrument and often not a very effective one in determining for whom, when, and where the criminalization of coercive control might be of benefit. In response to the bluntness of this instrument, debates have ensued focusing on improved legal definitions of coercive control, better methods of counting incidents of coercive control, improved training for criminal justice professionals in understanding and identifying coercive control, and better ways of gathering evidence on the presence of coercive control. (See, inter alia, Brennan and Myhill, 2021; Brennan et al., 2021; Barlow et al., 2020). Finessing law and practice in this way will, over time, lead to improvements in criminal justice practitioner responses to and understandings of coercive control both as an offence and as a feature of everyday life. However, nuanced attention to implementation processes may deal with some features of the implementation gap, what initiatives such as these cannot address is the conceptual gap (Lewis and Greene, 1978). It is within the conceptual gap that a fundamental challenge to the drive to criminalize coercive control lies.

To be more specific, the embrace of the law as a response to domestic abuse in general as well as coercive control in particular also equates with an embrace of governing through crime. It is at this level that one layer of the unintended consequences, which are the focus of this chapter, lie. Goodmark (2018) and others have pointed out, and has been stated above, for some women this turn to the criminal law as a response to intimate partner abuse has resulted in greater state control over them and their children's lives. For example, Stubbs and Wangmann (2015) cogently argue that the different legal domains occupied particularly by marginalized women requires them to perform themselves differently as women to comply with the expectations of these different authorities' vision of what constitutes them as a legitimate victim. Women are expected to do this to secure legal redress and safety for themselves and their children (see also McCulloch et al., 2020; Meyer, 2011). The implied point being that these expectations, and the practices they engender, also constitute a form of coercive control. This is in addition to the well-documented phenomenon that for some women, engagement with the law adds to their risk of arrest when the police officer arrests both the 'perpetrator' and the 'victim' in the absence of evidence easily differentiating one from the other (see Miller and Meloy, 2006; Nancarrow, 2019; Reeves, 2020). Moreover, many of these policies have had a differential effect on women of colour (Goodmark, 2018). As Balfour (2021: 10) states:

> Spiralling rates of the incarceration of Indigenous women in the decades that have followed the expansive carceral response to domestic violence are compelling evidence of the perils of these reforms.

The differential impact of a range of policies in relation to violence against women on marginalized and ethnic minority women was demonstrated by the work of Berk et al. (1992) when revisiting the efficacy of mandatory arrest policies. Nevertheless, despite this and a wide range of other evidence pointing to the contested and sometimes dubious value of criminal justice responses, this kind of response, as a focus of activity, has proceeded apace across the globe. While some of this activity can be attributed to what Goodmark (2015) has called 'exporting without a licence', some must also be attributed to the rather unholy alliance between feminist advocacy and the governing through crime agenda associated with neo-liberalism. Part of that agenda has been to make claims in relation to domestic abuse as something all women are subjected to. As Bumiller (2008: 157) has observed, while it was important to recognize that abuse occurs among all women regardless of age, class, ethnicity, and so on:

> this rhetorical framing of the problem obfuscates the reality that a woman's risk for sexual violence in all forms is highly dependent on her social identity, status, and circumstances: the most likely victim is female, black, unmarried, poor, and living alone or with children in an urban area.

It is at this juncture that the tensions between advocacy, the law and practice come to the fore. It is also at this juncture that the rather more invisible features of the recourse to the law, despite its own coercive tendencies, also become more visible.

The drive to criminalize coercive control may have reached out across (at least) the Anglo-speaking globe, but Lacey (2013) reminds us any process of criminalization is actually more complex than simply introducing a new law. While policy initiatives appear to travel the globe with haste (on this in relation to violence against women see Walklate and Fitz-Gibbon, 2018, among others) and that these appears to suggest global policy convergence, significant local institutional and political-economic frameworks are also in play. (See several of the contributions in Carrington et al., 2018). Further to understanding the importance of local context, Lacey (2016) goes on to observe that the law in action is not the same as the law in books (as the problems of implementing coercive control laws referred to above illustrate, see also Walklate, 2008). Importantly, Lacey (2016: 18) states:

> A primary gatekeeper between social behaviour which might be defined as criminal and the process of formal criminalisation is the ordinary citizen. What this implies, among other things, is that where central, hierarchically defined criminal law standards depart from community standards – as, unfortunately, has often been the case in relation to the application of the law of assault to domestic violence … Lack of alignment with community-based control will, therefore, place limits on the effectiveness with which centrally determined hierarchically imposed regulatory objectives can be pursued: in this sense, wider social norms themselves regulate formal criminalisation.
>
> (Lacey, 2016: 18)

These observations are telling. First, they serve to remind us of the tensions documented elsewhere is this book of the question of when does compliance in a relationship become coercive, how that might be recognized by the parties concerned, and how it might come to be understood as criminal. In some respects these are the questions similarly posed by Mooney (2007) some time ago concerning the persistence of violence against women as a private common-place while seemingly a public anathema. Thus, from a point of view, the drive to criminalize coercive control fails to take account of the role and importance of the 'ordinary citizen' in the policy process. By implication this lends some weight to problematizing criminalization as a 'solution' to violence against women (see also Goodmark, 2018). Second, the analysis proffered by Lacey (2016) implies caution in relation to the recourse to law because of the ways in which neoliberal political economies in particular serve to frame such debates: governing through crime. As was suggested in earlier chapters, this observation encourages some deeper thinking about the contextual origins of defining coercive control as a 'liberty crime' and the relevance of such a definition to other jurisdictions. Finally, Lacey's work stresses the importance of placing any understanding of criminalization within the wider context of the role and function of the criminal law itself. In adding these layers of complexity to understanding criminalization, Lacey's work inexorably draws attention to how the notion of criminal responsibility is understood (who is responsible for doing what to whom) which ultimately leads to a consideration of who is deemed responsible in law. Put more simply: who the subject of law is.

To appreciate the nature of criminalization and its links with the responsible subject of law, Lacey (2016: 16) argues that the processes of criminalization need to be placed within a 'regulatory space' occupied by different actors (for example, criminal justice professionals, non-governmental organizations, individuals, and private security companies), all of whom are involved in standard setting, monitoring and enforcing the criminal law. All of these actors and the institutions in which they operate can be differently organized with different priorities. Thus, by definition, the process of criminalization is frequently incomplete and contested. Nevertheless, it is through these processes that the responsible subject of law is constructed and reconstructed; that is gains legitimacy. This legitimacy ultimately serves the interests of the state. Two further questions remain: what the relevance of the introduction of this level of complexity is in responding to coercive control and what relevance it also has for the drive to criminalize coercive control. These two issues are themselves interconnected as will be developed below.

Coercive control, the man of law, and the responsible subject of law

Recognition of the complexities of criminalization means recognizing that the recourse to law affords the opportunity for consequences above and beyond the symbolic power of the law. Lacey's work encourages an appreciation of two issues. First, it encourages more nuanced thinking about the slippages between law in theory and law in practice (alluded to above) and directs attention to issues above and beyond better education and training of criminal justice professionals for example. Second, it creates the space in which to appreciate what factors mitigate against the law's ability to work in a hierarchical fashion, that is change behaviour.

To return to basics for a moment, the process of criminalization creates complainants and defendants (victims and offenders). Complainants and defendants are mutually co-existent: each brought into being by the criminal law. In law, defendants and complainants are intimately connected as legal subjects by legal understandings of responsibility and relatedly constructions of responsibilite subjects (of law). These responsible subjects are gendered (Lacey, 2013). Thus, in law, understandings of who did what to whom and why are interconnected and gendered. This fundamental framing of the complainant and defendant reveals much about the limitations of looking to changing the law per se as offering the means through which to change behaviour, particularly if that recourse to law fails to understand the gendered constructions of who is responsible for what, on which the criminal law is based.

Of course, it is the case that understandings of criminal responsibility have changed over time (Lacey, 2016) and there are different ways in which the person of law with responsibilities can be constructed (Naffine, 2003). Nevertheless, some features of this person of law persist over and through time (Lacey, 2013), particularly in relation to gender. Moreover, while it is the case that some laws can, and do, specifically include gendered understandings of certain behaviours (as the Scottish coercive control legislation does, hence its label as the 'gold standard' of such legislation, Scott, 2020), the delivery of decisions within the law in terms of gendered notions of responsibility have changed little. For Lacey (2007) being deemed responsible (in law) and being judged responsible (in law) refract the enduring presumption that the responsible subject of law is the entrepreneurial, rational, white, male (Naffine, 1990). This presumption frames the responsible subject of law in both national and international law and permeates understandings of, and responses to, both complainants and defendants (victims and offenders). This gendered subject impacts on women's experiences of the law in myriad ways, including coercive control, and arguably is most transparent in cases of lethal violence in which the woman is the defendant. This observation returns us to the potentiality of coercive control as a mitigation in cases of lethal violence raised by the case of Sally Challen discussed in Chapter 4.

One way of putting the Challen case in the broader context of the responsible subject is to reflect upon the work of Ballinger (2016). She revisited the case of Ruth Ellis, the last woman to be hanged for murder in the UK. The guilty verdict in this case was appealed (unsuccessfully) in 2003, and Ballinger considers both the grounds for this appeal and its outcome. The appeal was rejected on two grounds, the second of which is pertinent to the concerns of this chapter. This was the undeniable admission made by Ellis. Ellis, when asked what she intended to do with the gun in her possession, she replied that she intended to kill him (her partner). She maintained this until her execution. For Ballinger (2016) this case still provokes considerable interest because of the court's response in overemphasizing Ellis' admission of responsibility and underemphasizing Blakely's (her victim) irresponsibility towards her. In doing this, the court took the concept of responsibility itself as being neutral and given. However, as Ballinger (2016) argues, such neutrality was misplaced. Ellis and Blakely belonged to different social classes, were clearly differently committed to their relationship, with Blakely clearly having considerable power and influence over Ellis because of his alleged use of psychological and physical violence throughout their relationship. It takes little effort to see the resonances between some features of this case and that of Sally Challen. Nevertheless, the legal desire to assign individual responsibility for what took place meant that the complexities of the case, as outlined by Ballinger, were rendered invisible. This was assisted by Ellis' own admission. (In the case of Sally Challen the outcome of her appeal case and the court's resistance to seeing the complexities of coercive control was also aided by the decision on her part to take the weapon with which she killed her husband with in her handbag). As observed by Midson (2016), the complex narratives of people's lives became transformed into a simple legal one: who was responsible for what.

Thus complex lives become manageable and controllable through the law and are simultaneously sanitized into something resembling 'normal' (heterosexual) relationships (Dawson, 2016), which are thereby made intelligible in law. This search for gendered, individualized, responsibility occurs in international courts too (Houge, 2016) and while in people's real lives responsibility might well be multi-layered, complex, and complicated, in law this responsible subject is constituted by whatever means possible as a neoliberal, governable, gendered, subject (O'Malley, 2010) or as Bumiller (2008: 97) might say of women subjected to these processes:

> these women often have no choice but to be dependent on the state to escape the violence encountered in their private lives. In efforts to redress violation or as refugees from domestic violence, these 'victims' enter into a perilous involvement with the penal/welfare state. Thrust into new relationships within the public sphere, women often find that they experience brutalities that mimic the violence they hoped to leave behind.

Or further, as Gribaldo (2021) argues, these 'unexpected subjects' of law present the courts with '(un)familiar violence' in every sense of these words. The import of Bumiller's (2008) observation is developed more fully below but at this juncture it is sufficient to say that the responsible subject of law and its (in)visible presence marginalizes the status of women as subjects of law and the complexity of their lives which, when under the legal microscope are sure to be silenced along with their gender (Gerard and Kerr, 2016).

So, gender frames how the legal process responds to complainants and defendants (victims and offenders) and informs how they are constructed as responsible (neoliberal) subjects (Lacey, 2016). These are not new observations, but they are absent from the recent debates to expand the remit of the criminal law to capture coercive and controlling behaviours. The failure to recognize the silent but pervasive influence of the responsible subject in this recourse to law is both telling and important for (at least) two reasons. This influence brings into view the question of who the subject of criminalization is, and also whose interests are served in the construction of this subject.

Coercive control, responsible subjects, and blameless victims

Some time ago, Mills (1999) documented the myriad ways in which the state replicated the abuses experienced by abused women. These ranged from failing to hear her and/or rejecting her views to taking away her freedom when she (the victim) turned abuser. In a different, though parallel analysis, Douglas (2018) has referred to the ways in which the legal system itself facilitates the further abuse of by a partner. She calls this 'legal system abuse' and she goes on to consider the ways in which criminalizing coercive control might afford further possibilities for the proliferation of such abuse, especially when hearings are contested. In recounting women's experiences of the legal process, she further contests:

> Their engagement with law was often extended, and sometimes driven, by their abusers who hunted, battled, and played with them through law.
>
> (Douglas, 2021: 88)

Mills (1999) was talking about the system itself as abusive, especially in the pursuit and adoption of mandatory policies of intervention. The consequences of this have been demonstrated by Edwards (2012), as illustrated in the practices of compelling reluctant victims (often fearful abused women) to give evidence. Douglas (2021) is talking about the system facilitating the further abuse by abusive partners. As Douglas' (2021) recent work demonstrates there is more to be said about this kind of system-generated abuse when women's fear of the legal process is set alongside the fear of their partners. Arguably, these fears become more acute the more marginal the woman is.

It has already been stated above that the interplay of the penal-welfare complex adds to the fears that women with children face when encountering these services in relation to being judged as a 'good' mother or not (Maher et al., 2021). These fears are overlaid for women with disabilities. For example, for women living with disabilities 'because of prevailing stereotypes about their capability as parents and ... because removal of children from parents with disabilities happens at a much higher rate' (Victorian Royal Commission on Family Violence, 2016; 31, 183), their fears can, and are, compounded. Moreover, as Wilson (2017: 288) reports,

> The under-reporting of family violence for indigenous peoples is a concern made worse by structural discrimination, fear of being excluded from their community, fears about consequences for the offender, lack of access to services due to rurality and remoteness, and encountering culturally inappropriate responses.

This silencing contributes further to women 'feeling unsafe within one's family and within a system designed to provide helping services can place indigenous women and children at greater risk of serious injury and death' (Wilson, 2017: 289). As a result the coercive and controlling behaviour of a partner may be seen as more tolerable when compared with the coercive and controlling responses of the state and its authorities (Wilson, 2020; see also Nancarrow, 2019).

Put simply, for women victim-survivors – for whom the state and/or their family are feared more than their partner – to engage 'successfully' with the criminal justice system and its processes, they must demonstrate that they are blameless victims. This is a system-driven requirement. Only blameless victims can challenge the powerful effects and consequences of the gendered responsible subject of law. Returning to the Sally Challen case, this is again illustrative of the power of these processes. Given the complex nature of people's real lives and relationships, particularly where coercive and controlling behaviour has been a feature, to be constituted as a blameless victim in the processes that such relationships engender is a significant challenge indeed. As Walklate and Fitz-Gibbon (2021: 9) suggest:

> As some of the evidence in relation to criminal justice responses to intimate partner violence already illustrates, the reality is that

the state finds it much easier to construct women as dual offenders than it does to readily accept and legitimise their status as a victim-survivor.

To summarize, gender continues to pervade struggles to interpret and/ or reform the criminal law. The failure to take account of the pervasive influence of gender, is likely to result in the continued repetition of past mistakes which are unlikely to meet the needs of women victim-survivors (Smart, 1989; Hanna, 2009).

Indeed, history reveals that reforms are just as likely to serve the needs of men, in contradiction to their intended purpose (Smart, 1989). Gender continues to be pervasive in this way because the criminal law and its operation is intimately connected with the construction of governable (responsible) subjects in the interests of law and order. This process thrives on maintaining public and private violence(s) as separate and separable (as Gribaldo, 2021, might say, as '(un)familiar violence' for which individuals can be responsible over whom the state has the power to punish). The construction of blameless victims is essential to this bigger project. The project to criminalize coercive control not only overlooks these issues, but it is also silent on them. The question remains; how might it be possible to move beyond this kind of impasse? Untying the (un)happy marriage between feminist advocacy, criminalization and, law and order politics carries costs (Bumiller, 2008) but is not without potentialities. One way of thinking about these potentialities is to revisit the different ways in which coercive control can be understood as discussed in the introduction of this book.

Concluding thoughts

Responding to coercive control: the challenges of thinking differently

The introductory chapter to this book suggested four differently emphasized conceptualizations of coercive control; the clinical/psychological, the gendered, the social, and the legal. As previous chapters have highlighted, these different emphases draw attention to the different possibilities of understanding and responding to coercive control. As had also been demonstrated these different emphases are not mutually exclusive, they are all differently contested, and they each contain within them different inclusions and exclusions. Of course, it is important to note that while this book has been concerned to critically assess the efficacy of each of these conceptualizations, this has not and does not imply that experiences of coercive control do not exist or are not hugely impactive on those who experience them. However, in acknowledging the import of coercive control questions remain concerning, what kind of policy intervention might best make a difference to those whose lives are marked by these kinds of experiences. Each of the different understandings of coercive control reiterated above imply differently emphasized points of intervention.

To elucidate: the clinical/psychological emphasis found in the work of Stark (2007) clearly places importance on practitioners' capabilities to listen to and contextualize what victim-survivors of coercive control are telling them. This clearly has implications for all those working in domestic abuse support services whether their role is in one to one therapeutic support, an independent domestic violence advisor or a frontline police officer. Indeed the frequently observed empirical finding from victim-survivors to be listened to would endorse this requirement from all who may be made aware of their circumstances. This would include health professionals, school-teachers, and family and friends. Being listened to can be the first step for victim-survivors in moving forward on their own course of action if action is what they choose to engage in. Equally important, of course, is that action does not always or even necessarily follow. Therefore not being judged by all these same people for not taking action is also important. This all stems from listening. Such listening may require improved training and awareness for all the professionals victim-survivors may come into contact with. To improve the lives of women living with coercive control, listening is not only important it might be enough.

This gendered emphasis found within coercive control viewed as a point of intervention might consider men as the focus of activity (not women) and would lead down policy routes much more in line with keeping the accountability of the offender in view (Spencer, 2016). Of course, as some of the discussion in Chapter 3 has illustrated, while women might comprise the majority of victims of coercive control, men can also be found on the receiving end of such behaviours. Recognition of men as victims rather than perpetrators not only requires listening skills, as in the previous example, but also requires acknowledging that men's responses to these kinds of experiences are likely to be very differently informed and focused. This observation clearly overlaps with the social construction of coercive control; that is the way in which social processes and expectations include and exclude some groups as legitimate and illegitimate victims. Moreover, these same social constructions inform responses and intervention practices with those same legitimate/ illegitimate victims. Ensuring that professional agencies in particular run with practices uncluttered by a range of assumptions associated with legitimate victim status (like good motherhood, for example, or views of dependency as with people with disabilities) constitutes a real challenge. Hester (2011) has referred to this as the 'three planets' model in which the competing frameworks of child protection, the family courts, and the criminal justice system constitute a difficult path for victim-survivors to navigate.

Put simply, there is a good deal of work that could be done to improve the lives of those living with coercive control in a range of different ways prior to and separate from whether these behaviours should or should not be criminalized and all the associated dilemmas that this route can result in. As this chapter and the previous chapter have indicated, the debates surrounding the criminalization of coercive control have captured the policy imagination in quite profound ways. The debate this has engendered, and the energy devoted to it, is in many ways remarkable. Moreover, as these two chapters have also endeavoured to demonstrate, the focus on the law comes with costs many of which are borne significantly by those least able to carry them: marginalized women. Yet, as this brief conclusion has suggested, there are different ways to think about how coercive control impacts on those subjected to it and different intervention routes that could be taken. Goodmark (2018) has crystallized some of this different thinking into an agenda which includes decriminalizing domestic violence. The pros and cons of that agenda per se is not the focus of concern here. However, what might be taken from Goodmark's position at this juncture is an appreciation that a more balanced approach to intimate partner abuse might serve the interests of victim-survivors in better and more meaningful ways.

References

Balfour G (2021) Decriminalizing domestic violence and fighting prostitution abolition: Lessons learned from Canada's anti-carceral feminist struggles. *International Journal for Crime, Justice and Social Democracy*. Advance online publication. https://doi.org/10.5204/ijcjsd.1993

Ballinger A (2016) A question of provocation or responsibility? Revisiting the case of Ruth Ellis and David Blakely. In Fitz-Gibbon K and Walklate S (Eds.) *Gender, homicide and responsibility: An international perspective* (pp. 13–35). Abingdon: Routledge.

Barlow C, Johnson J, Walklate S and Humphreys L (2020) Putting coercive control into practice: Problems and possibilities. *The British Journal of Criminology* 60(1): 160–179. https://doi.org/10.1093/bjc/azz041

Berk RA, Campbell A, Klap R and Western B (1992) The deterrent effect of arrest in incidents of domestic violence: A Bayesian analysis of four field experiments. *American Sociological Review 57*(5): 698–708. https://doi.org/ 10.2307/2095923

Brennan I and Myhill A (2021) Coercive control: Patterns in crimes, arrests and outcomes for a new domestic abuse offence. *The British Journal of Criminology*. https://doi.org/10.1093/bjc/azab072

Brennan I, Myhill A, Tagliaferi G and Tapley J (2021) Policing a new domestic abuse crime: effects of force-wide training on arrests for coercive control. *Policing and Society*. https://doi.org/10.1080/10439463.2020.1862838

Bumiller K (2008) *In an abusive state: How neoliberalism appropriated the feminist movement against sexual violence*. Durham, NC: Duke University Press.

Carrington K, Hogg R, Scott J and Sozzo M (Eds.) (2018) *The Palgrave handbook of criminology and the global south*. London: Palgrave.

Dawson M (2016) Representing intimacy, gender and homicide: The validity and utility of common stereotypes in law. In Fitz-Gibbon K and Walklate S (Eds.) *Gender, homicide and responsibility: An international perspective* (pp. 53–77). Abingdon: Routledge.

Douglas H (2018) Legal systems abuse and coercive control. *Criminology and Criminal Justice 18*(1): 84–99. https://doi.org/10.1177%2F1748895817728380

Douglas H (2021) *Women, intimate partner violence and the law*. Oxford; Oxford University Press.

Edwards S (2012) The duplicity of protection – prosecuting frightened victims: An act of gender-based violence. *The Journal of Criminal Law 76*(1): 29–52. 10.1350/jcla.2012.76.1.749.

Garland D (2001) *The culture of control*. Oxford; Oxford University Press.

Gerard A and Kerr T (2016) Lethal violence and legal ambiguities: Deaths in custody in Australia's offshore detention centres. In Fitz-Gibbon K and Walklate S (Eds.) *Gender, homicide and responsibility: An international perspective* (pp. 130–147). Abingdon: Routledge.

Goodmark L (2015) Exporting without license: The American attempt to end intimate partner abuse worldwide. In Goel R and Goodmark L (Eds.) *Comparative perspectives on gender violence: Lessons from efforts worldwide*. (pp. 3–14). Oxford: Oxford University Press.

Goodmark L (2018) *Decriminalizing domestic violence: A balanced policy approach to intimate partner violence*. Berkeley, CA: University of California Press.

Gribaldo A (2021) *Unexpected subjects: Intimate partner violence, testimony and the law*. Chicago, IL: Hau Books.

Hanna C (2009) The paradox of progress: Translating Evan Stark's coercive control into legal doctrine for abused women. *Violence Against Women 15*(12): 1458–1476.

Hester M (2011) The three planet model: Towards an understanding of contradictions in approaches to women and children's safety in contexts of domestic violence. *The British Journal of Social Work 41*(5): 837–853, https://doi.org/10.1093/bjsw/bcr095

Houge Bringedal A (2016) 'He seems to come out as a personally cruel person': Perpetrator re-presentations in direct murder cases at the ICTY. In

Fitz-Gibbon K and Walklate S (Eds.) *Gender, homicide and responsibility: An international perspective* (pp. 113–129). Abingdon: Routledge.

Lacey N (2007) Denial and responsibility. In Chinkin C, Downes D, Gearty C and Rock P (Eds.) *Crime, social control and human rights* (pp. 255–269). Cullompton, Devon: Willan Publishing. http://dx.doi.org/10.2139/ssrn.2126532

Lacey N (2013) The rule of law and the political economy of criminalisation: An agenda for research. *Punishment & Society 15*(4): 349–366. https://doi.org/10.1177/1462474513500619

Lacey N (2016) *In search of criminal responsibility*. Oxford: Oxford University Press.

Lewis R and Greene JR (1978) Implementation evaluation: A future direction in project evaluation. *Journal of Criminal Justice 6*(2): 167–176.

Maher JM, Fitz-Gibbon K, Meyer S, Roberts S and Pfitzner N (2021) Mothering through and in violence: Discourses of the 'good mother'. *Sociology*. https://doi.org/10.1177/0038038520967262

McCulloch J, Maher J, Walklate S, McGowan J, Fitz-Gibbon K (2020) Justice perspectives of women with disability: An Australian story. *International Review of Victimology*. https://doi.org/10.1177/0269758020906270

Meyer S (2011) Seeking help for intimate partner violence: Victims' experiences when approaching the criminal justice system for IPV-related support and protection in an Australian jurisdiction. *Feminist Criminology 6*(4): 268–290. https://doi.org/10.1177/1557085111414860

Midson B (2016) Coercive control and criminal responsibility: Victims who kill their abusers. *Criminal Law Forum 27*(4): 417–442. https://doi.org/10.1007/s10609-016-9292-5

Miller S and Meloy M (2006) Women's use of force: Voices of women arrested for domestic violence. *Violence against Women 12*: 89–115. https://doi.org/10.1177/1077801205277356

Mills L (1999) Killing her softly: Intimate abuse and the violence of state intervention. *Harvard Law Review 113*(2): 550–613. https://doi.org/10.2307/1342332

Mooney J (2007) Shadow values, shadow figures: Real violence. *Critical Criminology 15*: 159–170. https://doi.org/10.1007/s10612-007-9023-7

Naffine N (1990) *Law and the sexes*. London: Allen and Unwin.

Naffine N (2003) Who are law's persons? From Cheshire cats to responsible subjects. *Modern Law Review 66*(3): 346–367. https://doi.org/10.1111/1468-2230.6603002

Naffine N (2019) *Criminal law and the man problem*. London: Hart Publishing.

Nancarrow H (2019) *Unintended consequences of domestic violence law: Gendered aspirations and racialised realities*. Hampshire: Palgrave MacMillan.

O'Malley P (2010) Resilient subjects: Uncertainty, warfare and liberalism. *Economy and Society 39*(4): 488–509. https://doi.org/10.1080/03085147.2010.510681

Reeves E (2020) Family violence, protection orders and systems abuse: Views of legal practitioners, *Current Issues in Criminal Justice 32*(1): 91–110. https://doi.org/10.1080/10345329.2019.1665816

Royal Commission into Family Violence (2016) Report and *recommendations*. Melbourne: Royal Commission into Family Violence (Victoria).

Scott M (2020) The making of the new 'gold standard': The Domestic Abuse (Scotland) Act 2018. In McMahon M and McGorrery P (Eds.) *Criminalising coercive control: Family violence and the criminal law* (pp. 176–194). Singapore: Springer.

Simon J (2006) *Governing through crime: How the war on crime transformed American democracy and created a culture of fear*. New York, NY: Oxford University Press.

Smart C (1989) *Feminism and the power of law*. London: Routledge.

Spencer P (2016) Strengthening the web of accountability: Criminal courts and family violence offenders. *Alternative Law Journal 41*(4): 225.

Stark E (2007) *Coercive control: How men entrap women in personal life*. Oxford: Oxford University Press.

Stubbs J and Wangmann JM (2015) Competing conceptions of victims of domestic violence within legal processes. In Wilson D and Ross S (Eds.) *Crime, victims and policy* (pp. 107–132). Palgrave Macmillan. http://dx.doi.org/10.2139/ssrn.2627260

Walklate S (2008) What is to be done about violence against women? *British Journal of Criminology 48*(1): 39–54. https://doi.org/10.1093/bjc/azm050

Walklate S and Fitz-Gibbon K (2018) Criminology and the violence(s) of Northern Theorizing: A critical examination of policy transfer in relation to violence against women from the global north to the global south. In Carrington K, Hogg R, Scott J and Sozzo M (Eds.) *The Palgrave handbook of criminology and the global south* (pp. 847–865). London: Palgrave.

Walklate S and Fitz-Gibbon K (2021) Why criminalise coercive control? The complicity of the criminal law in punishing women through furthering the power of the state. *International Journal for Crime, Justice and Social Democracy*. Advance online publication. https://doi.org/10.5204/ijcjsd.1829

Wilson D (2017) Indigenous populations and the domestic homicide review process. In Dawson M (Ed.) *Domestic homicides and death reviews* (pp. 287–316). London: Palgrave-Macmillan.

Wilson D (2020) *Colonisation, race and coercive control*. Paper presented at Criminalizing Coercive Control Webinar, de Montford University, 30–31 July 2020.

6 Concluding thoughts

Coercive control, victim-survivors, and the policy process

Introduction

The purpose of this book has been to introduce the reader to the contested concept of coercive control and its potential for translation into the criminal law. Throughout this discussion, the powerful and impactive presence of coercive control as a feature of interpersonal relationships has been made clear. However, what has also been made clear in the coverage offered are the difficulties associated with acknowledging that presence and the translation of its recognition into policy. Over the last ten years, this translation (of coercive control) has focused on the role of the law as a response in several jurisdictions and some of the issues associated with this have been the focus of earlier chapters in this book. Of course, there are ways, other than the criminal law, that coercive control can be recognized and responded to in relation to professional practice. However, in many ways, in relation to policy debates, the voices in favour of criminalization, that is finding a role for the law, have dominated. In this conclusion, the aim is to reflect upon some features of both coercive control and this search for a role for the criminal law, within some wider processes which have been touched upon but have remained less visible in the discussion presented so far. The following three issues are developed below: the questions associated with policy transfer, finding a space for victim-survivor voices, and the search for holistic policy responses to domestic abuse. Each of these will be discussed in turn.

The problem of policy transfer

The problems and possibilities of policy transfer within criminal justice have been well documented (Sparks and Newburn, 2002; Jones and Newburn, 2006, 2013). Much of this work has proceeded keeping an

DOI: 10.4324/9781003019114-6

appreciation of the convergent tendencies within neo-liberalism in view (Garland, 2001), and much of it also points to the uneven nature of this process (O'Malley, 2002). Mediating factors for the success of policy transfer are made visible within this literature, notably, the importance of policy champions and implementation processes (Jones and Newburn, 2002), and the nature and influence of policy networks (Ryan et al., 2001). Importantly within this literature the role and influence of victim organizations and particular victim voices (Barker, 2007; Ginsberg, 2014; Walklate, 2016) is also apparent. Moreover, the alignment of some feminist voices with the law-and-order politics frequently associated with these neo-liberal developments has been commented on by Bumiller (2008) and the ways in which this alignment can do a disservice to some women has been discussed in some detail in Chapter 5. Moreover, it is already possible to discern, within the observations made so far, that policy responses taking account of coercive control have certainly benefitted from policy champions and policy networks. The development of the Scottish legislation stands as a good example of this (Scott, 2020), as do the ongoing debates concerning coercive control in different states in Australia.

More recently, the policy transfer context in relation to violence against women has been commented on by Goodmark (2015). As she observes, the global recourse to the law as a response to violence against women has been a dominant theme for some time despite the efficacy of this response having been subjected to considerable contestation (Smart, 1989; Walklate, 2008; Goodmark, 2012; Douglas, 2008). Nevertheless, such responses still capture political and policy imaginations, especially given the political import of being seen to be doing something (commented on in earlier chapters of this book). Moreover, the recourse to law response has been integral to international preoccupations with violence against women conjoining with human rights voices at the level of the United Nations, the European Union, and other regional organizations. Goodmark's (2015) critique of these developments in what she sees as the embedding of a US-oriented legal model into policy responses to woman abuse is telling. She labels this 'exporting without a licence' (Goodmark, 2015) and proceeds to comment that this embrace of the recourse to law fails to acknowledge the structural context in which abuse of women occurs in the United States and that this context challenges its efficacy for other contexts. In addition, this failure is compounded by the concomitant erasure of the importance of culture. Indeed, the importance of structure and culture in relation to understanding coercive control and its impact have been discussed in detail in Chapter 4. It has also been noted at several junctures in this book that the framing of coercive control as a 'liberty crime' by Stark (2007) speaks volumes about the socio-legal context from which he has drawn his observations. Indeed, it is notable that some countries embedded in different legal traditions have, or are thinking about, different styles of legal response and/or offences as ways of recognizing coercive control. In France and Denmark, for example, discussions have focused attention on specific offences of psychological abuse rather than coercive control itself, perhaps intimating that in evidential terms psychological abuse offers better options. Such developments notwithstanding, the presumptions underpinning the possibilities for travelling policies demand some reflection. As Cunneen and Rowe (2015: 15) pointedly observe:

> Eurocentric domestic violence, law and policy imposed in Indigenous contexts is often predicated on an incongruent ontological and epistemological reality – a reality based on the potential for autonomous and individualised decision making.

This echoes some of the concerns raised by Wilson (2020) in respect of coercive control commented on in earlier chapters.

The smoothing out of structure and culture embedded within the policy transfer process also brings with it the danger of silencing, that is the silencing of those voices for whom such policies are intended to help: women (see Hoyle, 1998; Chesney-Lind, 1998; Walklate, 2008; Walklate and Fitz-Gibbon, 2018). The embrace of the law alongside the liberal agenda of inclusion (Karstedt, 2013) assumed in the policy transfer process are also alluded to in Goodmark's (2015) analysis of 'exporting without a licence'. Yet, this liberal agenda of inclusion is problematic as was intimated in Chapter 5. In particular, the question of what happens to victim-survivor voices and the silencing of them in this process is one such problem and is the next theme to be discussed here.

Finding a space for victim-survivor voices

Of course, it has been increasingly evident over the last two decades that individual victim-survivor voices have made their presence felt in the political and policy arena both generally and in the specific field of family and domestic violence. Nowhere has this been more evident in recent years than in Australia, where Rosie Batty gained national recognition (as Australian of the Year in 2015) in speaking out on family violence after the murder of her son Luke by her ex-partner. How and why her voice came to be given space has been subjected to some detailed investigation by Wheildon et al. (2021) and Walklate et al. (2019). Both analyses differently draw upon Christie's (1986) concept of the ideal victim as one way of making sense of why she was listened to, with Wheildon et al. (2021) adding the concept of policy entrepreneur to their sense-making of this process. Interestingly their use of this concept adds some nuance to the notion of policy champions discussed above and it is indeed the case that Batty's voice had some influence over the Victorian Government's decision to establish a Victim Survivor's Advisory Council in 2016 in the aftermath of their Royal Commission on Family Violence. Moreover, while Batty's story provoked narratives of victimhood drawing attention to her as a heroic victim (Meyers, 2016), and while such individual voices have had an increasing presence in criminal justice policy-making, (for example, in New South Wales the commitment to criminalize coercive control has been presented in terms of having listened to victim-survivor voices), there are serious problems in taking these stories to stand for all victim/women's experiences. Further there are dangers in assuming that the voices which lend themselves most readily to the recourse to law reflect the experiences and voices of all victim-survivors. Such voices might have some value as 'moral beacons' (Brewer and Hayes, 2011), but importantly even those who become moral beacons are not necessarily listened to well and some are not listened to at all. This is particularly important when considering the strengths and limitations of the policy possibilities such voices give weight to.

This book has charted the growth and recognition of coercive control in the violence against women literature (work that has been historically rooted in women's own accounts of their lives) and the ways in which this growth has been harnessed in the push for criminalization. Interestingly, the push for criminalization has occurred on the back of individual stories (many of which are horrendous) and the voices of advocates claiming to speak for the women they support, but with little systematic evidence from the women (and others) subjected to coercive control as to their views on criminalization. This is indeed a thought-provoking lacuna given the widely documented evidence surrounding women's reluctance, when living with violence, to engage with the criminal justice system (Hoyle and Sanders, 2000; Buzawa, Buzawa and Stark, 2017; Nancarrow, 2019). Some work has considered how women manage coercive control in their relationships (see, inter alia, Bruton and Tyson, 2018) and much is known about how women manage living with violence more generally (Genn, 1988; Kirkwood, 1993). Indeed, some recent work by Douglas and Fitzgerald (2020) on the offence of non-fatal strangulation illustrates how the law might be framed to take women's views into account. In the light of the evidence discussed in Chapter 5, taking some account of where, when, and how women's fears of state intervention take precedence over their fears of their partners is certainly worthy of further consideration within the push to criminalize coercive control. Put more simply, the absence of a similar evidence base, to the one used to recognize coercive control (victim-survivor experiences) is telling. Of course, the law cannot be ignored as a space in which there are possibilities for furthering women's safety. However, as Douglas' (2021) recent empirically based exploration of women's experiences of the law as seen through their eyes demonstrates, there is much more that can be done. Finding a place for the law is the last theme to be discussed here.

The search for holistic policy responses

In a study, similarly focused to that of Douglas (2021), Gribaldo (2021) asks:

> How can you be true to yourself and your own deepest feelings (love, suffering, intimacy) without being judged for your own condition?
>
> (Ibid: 127)

In many ways, this is a question which has reared its head on more than one occasion throughout this book. It is a very pertinent question when reflecting on the messy relationship between women's real lives, the presence of violence(s) within it, and the search for policy responses. As Gribaldo (2021: 125–126) notes, these lives and their violence(s) cannot 'speak for themselves', since they come from a subjectivity that does not quite match with socio-legal demands. She goes on to suggest that such violence(s) cannot be told because, even when there are witnesses to tell the story, they tell a story which is already known. Neighbours know. Families know. Friends know. Such knowing may be known and unknown all at the same time, but if the term 'space for action' (Sharp-Jeffs et al., 2018) means anything much at all, then it arguably begins in these spaces. It is the case that even within the most horrendous incidents of family violence which have been used in calls to criminalize coercive control (Fitz-Gibbon et al., 2020), the intention of the perpetrator was known by his friends and his previous behaviour was known by family members. In searching for a differently emphasized nuance for a criminal justice response that evades the problems for women eloquently expressed by Gribaldo (2021), keeping the perpetrator in view and accountable (Spencer, 2016) might be a place in which the wider public has a role alongside criminal justice. Importantly, the absence of a public discourse focusing attention on victim-survivor views on safety and unsafety is also central to such a re-orientation (Stanko, 1900; Wilson et al., 2019). These observations, of course, take us into the realms of debates not directly relevant to the contents of this book. However, the point is well made. Without more holistic considerations that shift attention from the victim-survivor and her behaviour, behaviour which proves to be so problematic for social-legal responses and the 'three planets' (Hester, 2011) to which women are subjected often as part of the socio-legal response, then the recourse to the criminal law through the criminalization of coercive control, will inevitably result in furthering the power of the state to punish women. (Walklate and Fitz-Gibbon, 2021).

References

Barker V (2007) The politics of pain: A political institutionalist analysis of crime victims' moral protests. *Law and Society Review 41*(3): 619–663. https://doi.org/10.1111/j.1540-5893.2007.00316.x

Brewer J and Hayes B (2011) Victims as moral beacons; victims and perpetrators in Northern Ireland. *Contemporary Social Science 6*(1): 73–88.

Bruton C and Tyson D (2018) Leaving violent men: A study of women's experiences of separation in Victoria, Australia. *Australian & New Zealand Journal of Criminology 51*(3): 339–354.

Bumiller K (2008) *In an abusive state: How neoliberalism appropriated the feminist movement against sexual violence.* Durham, NC: Duke University Press.

Buzawa CG, Buzawa ES and Stark E (Eds.) (2017) *Responding to domestic violence: The integration of criminal justice and human services (4th ed.).* Thousand Oaks, CA: SAGE Publications, Inc.

Chesney-Lind M (1998) Doing feminist criminology. *The Criminologist 13*(1):1–3.

Christie N (1986) The ideal victim. In Fattah EA (Ed.) *From crime policy to victim policy: Reorienting the justice system* (pp. 17–30). London: Palgrave Macmillan. https://doi.org/10.1007/978-1-349-08305-3_2

Cunneen C and Rowe S (2015) Decolonising indigenous victimisation. In Wilson D and Ross S (Eds.) *Crime, victims and policy: International contexts, local experiences* (pp. 10–32). London: Palgrave Macmillan.

Douglas H (2008) The criminal law's response to domestic violence: What's going on? *Sydney Law Review 30*: 439–469.

Douglas H (2021) *Women, intimate partner violence and the law.* Oxford: Oxford University Press.

Douglas H and Fitzgerald R (2020) Women's stories of non-fatal strangulation: Informing the criminal justice response. *Criminology & Criminal Justice.* doi:10.1177/1748895820949607

Fitz-Gibbon K, Walklate S and Meyer S (2020) Australia is not ready to criminalise coercive control. 1 October https://theconversation.com/australia-is-not-ready-to-criminalise-coercive-control-heres-why-146929

Garland D (2001) *The culture of control.* Oxford: Oxford University Press.

Genn H (1988) Multiple victimization. In Maguire M and Pointing J (Eds.) *Victims of crime: A new deal?* (pp. 90–100). Milton Keynes: Open University Press.

Ginsberg R (2014) Mighty crime victims: Victims' rights and neoliberalism in the American conjuncture. *Cultural Studies 28*(5–6): 911–946. https://doi.org/10.10 80/09502386.2014.886485

Goodmark L (2012) *A troubled marriage: Domestic violence and the legal system.* New York, NY: New York University Press.

Goodmark L (2015) Exporting without license: The American attempt to end intimate partner abuse worldwide. In Goel R and Goodmark L (Eds.) *Comparative perspectives on gender violence: Lessons from efforts worldwide* (pp. 3–14). Oxford: Oxford University Press.

Gribaldo A (2021) *Unexpected subjects: Intimate partner violence, testimony and the law.* Chicago, IL: Hau Books.

Hester M (2011) The three planet model: Towards an understanding of contradictions in approaches to women and children's safety in contexts of domestic violence. *The British Journal of Social Work 41*(5): 837–853. https://doi.org/10.1093/bjsw/bcr095

Hoyle C (1998) *Negotiating domestic violence.* Oxford: Clarendon Press.

Hoyle C and Sanders A (2000) Police response to domestic violence: From victim choice to victim empowerment? *British Journal of Criminology 4*(1): 14–36.

Jones T and Newburn T (2002) Policy convergence and crime control in the USA and the UK: Streams of influence and levels of impact. *Criminal Justice 2*(2): 173–204. https://doi.org/10.1177/17488958020020020401

Jones T and Newburn T (2006) *Policy transfer and criminal justice.* Maidenhead: Open University Press.

Jones T and Newburn T (2013) Policy convergence, politics and comparative penal reform: Sex offender notification schemes in the USA and UK. *Punishment & Society 15*(5): 439–467. https://doi.org/10.1177/1462474513504801

Karstedt S (2013) Democracy and the project in liberal inclusion. In Carrington K, Ball M, O'Brien E and Tauri J (Eds.) *Crime, justice and democracy: International perspectives* (pp. 16–33). London: Palgrave Macmillan.

Kirkwood C (1993) *Leaving abusive partners: From the scars of survival to the wisdom for Change.* London: Sage.

Meyers DT (2016) *Victims' stories and the advancement of human rights.* New York, NY: Oxford University Press.

Nancarrow H (2019) *Unintended consequences of domestic violence law: Gendered aspirations and racialised realities.* Hampshire: Palgrave MacMillan.

O'Malley P (2002) Globalising risk: Distinguishing styles of 'neo-liberal' criminal justice in Australia and the USA. *Criminal Justice 2*(2): 205–222. https://doi.org /10.1177/17488958020020020501

Ryan M, Savage S and Wall D (Eds.) (2001) *Policy networks in criminal justice.* London: Palgrave-MacMillan.

Scott M (2020) The making of the new 'gold standard': The Domestic Abuse (Scotland) Act 2018. In McMahon M and McGorrery P (Eds.) *Criminalising coercive control: Family violence and the criminal law* (pp. 176–194). Singapore: Springer.

Sharp-Jeffs N, Kelly L and Klein R (2018) Long journeys toward freedom: The relationship between coercive control and space for action-measurement and emerging evidence. *Violence against Women 24*(2): 163–185. doi: 10.1177/1077801216686199.

Smart C (1989) *Feminism and the power of law.* London: Routledge.

Sparks R and Newburn T (Eds.) (2002) How does crime policy travel? Special issue of *Criminal Justice 2*(2): 107–109. London: Palgrave Macmillan.

Spencer P (2016) Strengthening the web of accountability: Criminal courts and family violence offenders. *Alternative Law Journal 41*(4): 225.

Stanko B (1990) *Everyday violence.* London: Pandora.

Stark E (2007) *Coercive control: How men entrap women in personal life.* Oxford: Oxford University Press.

Walklate S (2008) What is to be done about violence against women? *British Journal of Criminology 48*(1): 39–54. https://doi.org/10.1093/bjc/azm050

Walklate S (2016) The metamorphosis of the victim of crime: From crime to culture and the implications for justice. *International Journal for Crime, Justice and Social Democracy 5*(4): 4–16. https://doi.org/10.5204/ijcjsd.v5i4.280

Walklate S and Fitz-Gibbon K (2018) Criminology and the violence(s) of Northern theorizing: A critical examination of policy transfer in relation to violence against women from the global north to the global south. In Carrington K, Hogg R, Scott J and Sozzo M (Eds.) *The Palgrave handbook of criminology and the global south* (pp. 847–865). London: Palgrave.

Walklate S, Maher J, McCulloch J, Fitz-Gibbon K and Beavis K (2019) Victim stories and victim policy: Is there a case for a narrative victimology? *Crime, Media, Culture 15*(2): 199–215.

Walklate S and Fitz-Gibbon K (2021) Why criminalise coercive control? The complicity of the criminal law in punishing women through furthering the power of the state. *International Journal for Crime, Justice and Social Democracy 15*(2): 199–215. https://doi.org/10.1177/1741659018760105

Wheildon LJ, True J, Flynn A and Wild A (2021) The batty effect: Victim-survivors and domestic and family violence policy change. *Violence against Women.* doi: 10.1177/10778012211024266.

Wilson D, Mikahere-Hall A, Sherwood J, Cootes K and Jackson D (2019) *E Tū Wāhine, E Tū Whānau: Wāhine Māori keeping safe in unsafe relationships.* Auckland, NZ: Taupua Waiora Māori Research Centre.

Wilson D (2020) *Colonisation, race and coercive control.* Paper presented at Criminalizing Coercive Control Webinar, de Montford University, 30–31 July 2020.

Index

For Product Safety Concerns and Information please contact our EU
representative GPSR@taylorandfrancis.com
Taylor & Francis Verlag GmbH, Kaufingerstraße 24, 80331 München, Germany

www.ingramcontent.com/pod-product-compliance
Lightning Source LLC
Chambersburg PA
CBHW060409290526
45791CB00002B/679